Monopoly Protection:
The 90-Minute Guide to Patents, Trademarks, Copyrights, and Trade Secrets

JOHN S. FERRELL, ESQ.

FOURTH EDITION

ALSO BY JOHN S. FERRELL

■ ■ ■

Patent *Pro Se:*
The Entrepreneur's Guide to Provisional Patent Applications

Inventor's Notebook
(The Perfect Place to Store Your Great Ideas)

ENDORSEMENTS

■ ■ ■

"John Ferrell is hands down the most insightful and innovative IP lawyer I have ever met. We've recommended him to countless of our most successful clients and have built the expanding monopoly that Strategic Coach enjoys entirely on the strategies, structures, and processes that John lays out in this book."

- Dan Sullivan, Strategic Coach, Inc.

"John has extensive experience in the patent and copyright law arena. He understands how to think strategically about how to increase the value of a company through patents and not just filing a patent for its own sake. If you want to understand how patents can increase your company's ultimate value then this is the book for you."

- Will Bunker, founder of Match.com

"Having worked with John Ferrell since the formative stages of Polycom, I've come to value his contribution as much more than just patent counsel. He sees through to the core of product differentiation and develops an intellectual property roadmap to provide strong protection from $0 - $1 billion in revenue."

- Brian L. Hinman, CEO of Mimosa Networks, Inc. and former CEO of 2Wire, Inc. and Polycom, Inc.

"A new company needs a reliable foundation for its patent and intellectual property strategy, and that's tough to find as the world is only getting more complex. The young Polycom had the luck to find John Ferrell, who helped us build a well-balanced IP program that has leveraged our existing skills and enhanced our capture of new opportunities. John understands the goals of a modern enterprise, and is thoughtful and accessible in developing their solutions. Whether you're looking to start something new, or to clean up and enhance what you've already got, you'll find this book a real page-turner (yes, a book on patents!) that amply rewards your time."

— Jeff Rodman, founder of Polycom

"John Ferrell has proven for me to be the 'guru' of business and legal advice and provided me the opportunity to play with the biggest companies in the world. Buy this book and get ready to succeed."

— Stephen Key, successful inventor and bestselling author of *One Simple Idea*

*Dedicated with love to my parents,
Paul and Jeanne, and to my children,
Ashley, Kristin, and Benjamin*

Copyright ©2003-2013 by John S. Ferrell, Esq.
Second Printing

All rights reserved. Printed in the United States of America. Except as permitted under the United States Copyright Act of 1976, no part of this publication may be reproduced or distributed in any form or by any means, or stored in a data base or retrieval system, without the prior written permission of the publisher.

All photography is used with permission of its owners.
Cover art by Jacqui Faye Design, www.jacquifayedesign.com.

ISBN 978-0-9743776-4-3

CONTENTS

INTRODUCTION	xi
CHAPTER ONE: Starting with a *Cool* Idea	1
What is Intellectual Property?	7
CHAPTER TWO: Every Discovery Ever Made	13
History of Patents	18
U.S. Patent and Trademark Office	24
CHAPTER THREE: Patents	29
Types of Patents	29
Utility Patents	29
Design Patents	30
Plant Patents	31
Provisional Patent Applications	31
What Can Be Patented?	37
Why Do Patents Matter?	45
Applying For Patents	47
CHAPTER FOUR: Trademarks	53
Selecting a Strong Trademark	58
Why Do Trademarks Matter?	61
CHAPTER FIVE: Copyrights	64
Why Do Copyrights Matter?	67
Mask Works	71
Ownership of Copyrights	72
Protecting Your Copyrights	74

CHAPTER SIX: Trade Secrets	76
Why Do Trade Secrets Matter?	81
"Morning-After Pill" for NDAs	83
Protecting Trade Secrets	86
CHAPTER SEVEN: Conclusion	91
Bundle of Rights	93
The Business Decision	94
Appendix	96
Non-Disclosure Agreement	96
Assignment of Copyright	102
Index	103
About the Author	111

INTRODUCTION TO THE FOURTH EDITION

■ ■ ■

Monopolies are such interesting constructs. Having the legal right to prevent others from using your invention, telling your story, or sharing your secret formula are just a few of the immensely valuable privileges that intellectual property monopoly protections allow. I have enjoyed a career centered on my passion for creating and building these monopolies. I continue to be fascinated by the diversity of and the extent to which government grants of patents, trademarks and copyrights can enable the radical re-engineering of competitive landscapes.

Welcome to the Fourth Edition of *Monopoly Protection: The 90-Minute Guide to Patents, Trademarks, Copyrights, and Trade Secrets*.[1] This book was written for the entrepreneur on the go, and intended to be a quick read, perhaps during the brief span of an average two-hour plane ride. The chapters are short, and my editors have liberally sprinkled in pictures and shadow boxes to keep the content approachable, even while being enjoyed with a favorite high-octane energy drink.

---

1 Formerly titled, Protecting Your Techknowledgy ©2003-2013.

This Fourth Edition was motivated in part by the Leahy-Smith America Invents Act (AIA) of 2011, which enacted some of the most sweeping changes to the American patent system in more than a half-century. In 2013, for example, the United States joined the rest of the world in becoming a first-to-file patent system. It's now a race to the patent office for inventors; patents will be awarded to the first inventor who files the patent, not the first to invent, as was previously the case.

Although fresh off the press, this book—like the rest of our legal system—is only one Supreme Court case or presidential signature away from becoming obsolete. The Fifth Edition is already in the works. If you have comments, edits, or stories you would like to share, please drop me an email at jsferrell@carrferrell.com. In the meantime, best wishes to you in pursuit of your own Monopoly.

John S. Ferrell, Esq.

Monopoly Protection:
The 90-Minute Guide to Patents, Trademarks, Copyrights, and Trade Secrets

■ CHAPTER ONE ■

STARTING WITH A *COOL* IDEA

Willis Haviland Carrier

Willis Haviland Carrier is probably touching your life as you're reading this. He most likely touches your life anywhere you go—at home, at the office, in the grocery store, in the most secluded areas of your home. You can't even get away from him in your car.

But his effects are even more far-reaching than your own world. According to political columnist Molly Ivins, if it hadn't been for Willis, "… the rates of drunkenness, divorce, brutality, and murder would be Lord knows how much higher.

STARTING WITH A *COOL* IDEA

Productivity rates would plunge 40 percent over the world; the deep-sea fishing industry would be deep-sixed; Michelangelo's frescoes in the Sistine Chapel would deteriorate; rare books and manuscripts would fall apart; deep mining for gold, silver, and other metals would be impossible; the world's largest telescope wouldn't work; many of our children wouldn't be able to learn; and in Silicon Valley, the computer industry would crash."

All because one man was trying to prevent ink from misaligning on print jobs. It is amazing how critical air-conditioning and heating systems can be. Good thing Willis had an understanding of engineering, entrepreneurship, and the importance of protecting intellectual property.

Ironically, Willis struggled tremendously in school, finally learning fractions by cutting apples into pieces. He was an introverted child, spending much of his youth in solitude on his parents' farm in the rural community of Angola, New York. Yet, from such a relatively isolated world, a genius sprang forth. But, it took a lot of hard work.

Despite Willis' slow academic progress, he earned a scholarship from Cornell University. In addition to studying electrical engineering, Willis learned the basis of being an entrepreneur from mowing lawns, stoking furnaces, and forming a co-op student laundry.

After graduation, Willis went to work for the Buffalo Forge

STARTING WITH A *COOL* IDEA

Company designing heating systems to dry coffee and lumber. He discovered how much heat air would hold as it blew across heated pipes. This information allowed Buffalo Forge to accurately estimate the heater surface area required for a given space, saving the company $40,000 in the first year alone.

Air-conditioning was invented to improve the printing alignment of colored inks.

Willis was quickly promoted to the head of Buffalo Forge's experimental engineering department and commissioned by the Sackett-Wilhelms Lithographing Company of Brooklyn to solve its plant's temperature and humidity problem. Heat and humidity fluctuations inside the plant had been causing the printing paper dimensions to alter and the colored inks to misalign.

One night, Willis was waiting on a platform in a Brooklyn train station, covered in a heavy blanket of fog, pondering the printing problem. He was struck by a flash of genius and realized the basic relationships between humidity, dew point, and temperature. Perhaps the fog lifted, too.

The next morning, Willis invented a device to regulate the plant's temperature using a low-pressure, centrifugal system to take in air through a filter and pass the air over coils containing a stable, non-toxic coolant. The system pumped the cooled and dehumidified air into the printing plant and vented the warm air circulating the printing equipment outdoors. In 1906, Willis patented the design for the world's first indoor air-conditioning under the name, "Apparatus for Treating Air."

There's that critical issue of intellectual property.

Despite the success of Willis' invention, the Buffalo Forge Company closed in 1914. Willis and six other engineers obtained $35,000 in capital, as well as the Buffalo Forge air-conditioning patents, and started Carrier Engineering Corporation. In 1921, Carrier unveiled the first air conditioner targeted for large indoor areas, particularly businesses. The company then turned to the consumer market. In 1928, Carrier introduced the Weathermaker, which controlled household air temperature.

Today, Carrier is the world's largest manufacturer of air conditioners, with sales exceeding $12.5 billion worldwide and a patent portfolio containing more than 2,200 U.S. patents. Carrier products can be found across the world. Air-conditioning is arguably one of the most important inventions of the twentieth century, greatly improving the health and comfort of billions of people worldwide.

It all started with a boy from a farm in Angola that had a pretty cool idea…and knowledge of the importance of intellectual property.

UNITED STATES PATENT OFFICE.

WILLIS H. CARRIER, OF BUFFALO, NEW YORK, ASSIGNOR TO BUFFALO FORGE COMPANY, OF BUFFALO, NEW YORK.

APPARATUS FOR TREATING AIR.

No. 808,897.   Specification of Letters Patent.   Patented Jan. 2, 1906.

Application filed September 16, 1904. Serial No. 224,758.

To all whom it may concern:

Be it known that I, WILLIS H. CARRIER, a citizen of the United States, residing at Buffalo, in the county of Erie and State of New York, have invented a new and useful Improvement in Apparatus for Treating Air, of which the following is a specification.

This invention relates to apparatus for treating air previous to its use for ventilating and heating buildings or for other commercial purposes—such as drying, refrigerating, &c.—and more particularly to air-purifying apparatus of that kind in which a liquid or solution in a finely-divided condition or atomized spray is introduced into a current of air to be treated, which is then caused to pass through a separator consisting of baffle-plates which intercept and separate from the air the particles of liquid, together with the solid impurities contained therein.

The object of the invention is to provide an efficient practical apparatus of simple construction which will thoroughly separate all solid impurities, floating particles, and noxious material from the air either with or without altering its temperature and humidity.

In the accompanying drawings, Figure 1 is a view, partly in elevation and partly in vertical section, of an apparatus for treating air embodying the invention. Fig. 2 is a fragmentary horizontal section, on an enlarged scale, of the separating device. Fig. 3 is a diagram of the separating device. Fig. 4 is a perspective view of one of the separator plates or elements. Figs. 5 and 6 are enlarged sections in different planes of one of the spray-nozzles detached.

Like letters of reference refer to like parts in the several figures.

M represents an air trunk, conduit, or casing, of galvanized iron or other suitable material, through which a current of air is caused to pass in a horizontal direction by a fan or other propelling device K, connected with the casing. In the casing M, preferably near its open intake or front end, is located a spraying device H for introducing water or any other suitable treating liquid or solution into the air passing through the casing. The spraying device may be of any suitable construction which will fill the adjacent portion of the casing with a finely divided or atomized spray of the liquid and cause an intimate contact and mixture thereof with all portions of the air-current. The spray device shown consists of a vertical head or pipe connected with a supply-pipe F and provided with spray-nozzles h of a well-known type, (shown in Figs. 5 and 6,) which impart a whirling or circular motion to the issuing liquid and produce a very fine spray or vapor.

In the casing in rear of the spray device is a separator through which the air is passed for eliminating or separating therefrom the solid particles of foreign matter or impurities, together with all or a portion of the water which was introduced into the air for cleansing it. The separator comprises a series of parallel baffle plates or elements, made of sheet metal or other suitable material, separated by intervening passages for the air and arranged in an upright position, which will be understood to mean either vertically or inclined, so that the liquid or moisture removed from the air can flow down the surface of the plates or elements. The separator elements are provided with oblique faces joined by upright bends or angles, so as to form a series of continuous, sinuous, or zigzag passages between the elements for the air, which in its passage is deflected from side to side and caused to impinge against the alternate faces of the opposite separator plates or elements. Each plate or element comprises a forward portion consisting of oblique faces i, joined by a simple upright bend or angle j, and a rear portion consisting of oblique faces f g, joined by upright bends or angles, which are provided with flanges or portions b c, which project outwardly and rearwardly from the plates or in a direction opposed to the direction of movement of the air and form recesses or gutters.

The separator plates or elements are preferably constructed as shown in the drawings, from which it will be seen that the front portion of each plate consists of a single section or piece which is bent at the angle j, while the other portion consists of separate sections or pieces riveted or otherwise joined with the front edge of each section projecting beyond the joint to form the flanges b and c.

An obvious modification of the construction would be to make each plate or element of a

No. 808,897. PATENTED JAN. 2, 1906.
W. H. CARRIER.
APPARATUS FOR TREATING AIR.
APPLICATION FILED SEPT. 16, 1904.

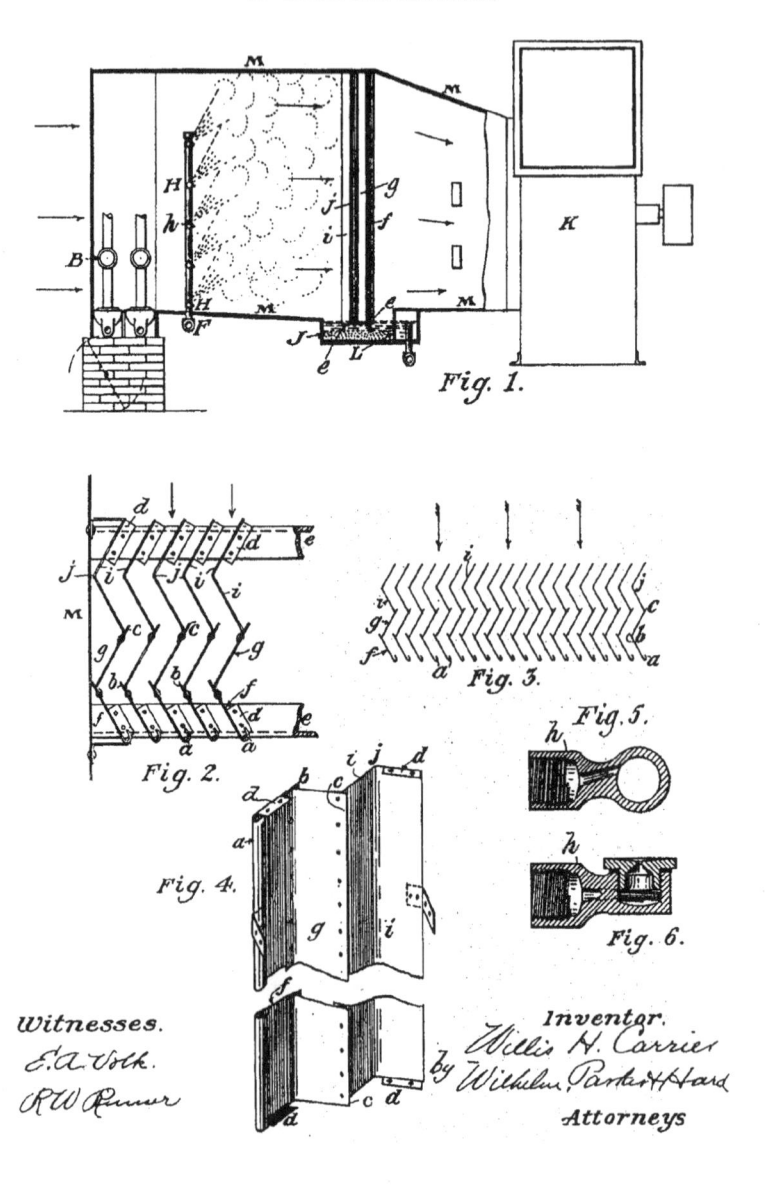

Fig. 1.

Fig. 2.

Fig. 3.

Fig. 4.

Fig. 5.

Fig. 6.

Witnesses.
E. A. Volk.
R. W. Renner.

Inventor.
Willis H. Carrier
by Wilhelm, Parker & Hard
Attorneys

WHAT IS INTELLECTUAL PROPERTY?

Hundreds of thousands of entrepreneurs over the past century have followed in the inventive footsteps of Willis Carrier. Starting with creative ideas and dreams, entrepreneurs have built great products, great companies, and great industries. But in order to protect the manifestations of those ideas and dreams, they also had to know how to protect the ingenuity behind it all.

> Intellectual property is the byproduct of creative thought.

This valuable creativity is often referred to in legal terms as intellectual property (IP). Intellectual property is the byproduct of creative thought. It is said to be intangible property in the sense that we cannot touch it or grow crops on it, but the property can be described, measured, valued, sold and traded as surely as a plot of land or a piece of jewelry. Intellectual property can consist of designs for machines, chemical formulas, software programs, methods of doing business, industrial designs, artistic works, books, music compositions, screenplays, blueprints, and just about anything else of value that results from intellectual creation.

> "... promote the Progress of Science and useful Arts ..."

The value of protecting intellectual property in the U.S. was recognized by the ingenious framers of the Constitution who granted to Congress special Constitutional authority to "... promote the Progress of Science and useful Arts, by securing for limited Times to Authors and Inventors the exclusive Right to their respective Writings and Discoveries."[1]

From the authority and powers that the framers granted under the Constitution, Congress provides the public with a set of protections that give monopoly rights to those who create and use valuable intellectual property. (Ben Franklin could now freely fly a kite in a lightning storm and not worry about somebody else stealing his unique method for harvesting electricity. That is, if he utilized the protections he helped to create.) For such purposes, there are at least four broad protections accessible to owners of intellectual property in the U.S., with each covering different aspects of a creative idea or invention. These protections include patents, trademarks, copyrights, and trade secrets.

Trademarks protect a company's goodwill.

However, the type of protection an inventor or creator may need varies with the creation. One, or a combination of several, may be required to comprehensively protect an idea or invention. Generally, trademarks protect a company's goodwill, copyrights protect creative expression, trade secret rights protect

---

1   U.S. Const. art. I, § 8, cl. 8.

company secrets that provide some business advantage to the company, and patents protect useful and ornamental inventions. Although these protections are different from one another, it is possible for a single creative work to be covered by more than one protective right. For example, a common bottle of Coca-Cola soft drink is covered by each of the four intellectual property rights.

According to the United States Patent and Trademark Office (USPTO), Coke's recipe is America's most famous trade secret. Coca-Cola, Inc. also holds numerous trademarks for its Coke product, including the labels on their bottles, cans, and apparel. The notoriety of Coke's trademark is evidenced by the fact that it was the first U.S.-issued trademark to appear in Moscow, Russia. The shape of the Coke bottle has also been the subject of several design patents, and the bottle label design, as well as the vast array of advertisements run by Coca-Cola, are all copyrighted.

Of course, an inventor or creator may not need each of these protections, but it would be wise to have the knowledge of each and the functions they serve.

One of America's most famous trademarks.

STARTING WITH A *COOL* IDEA

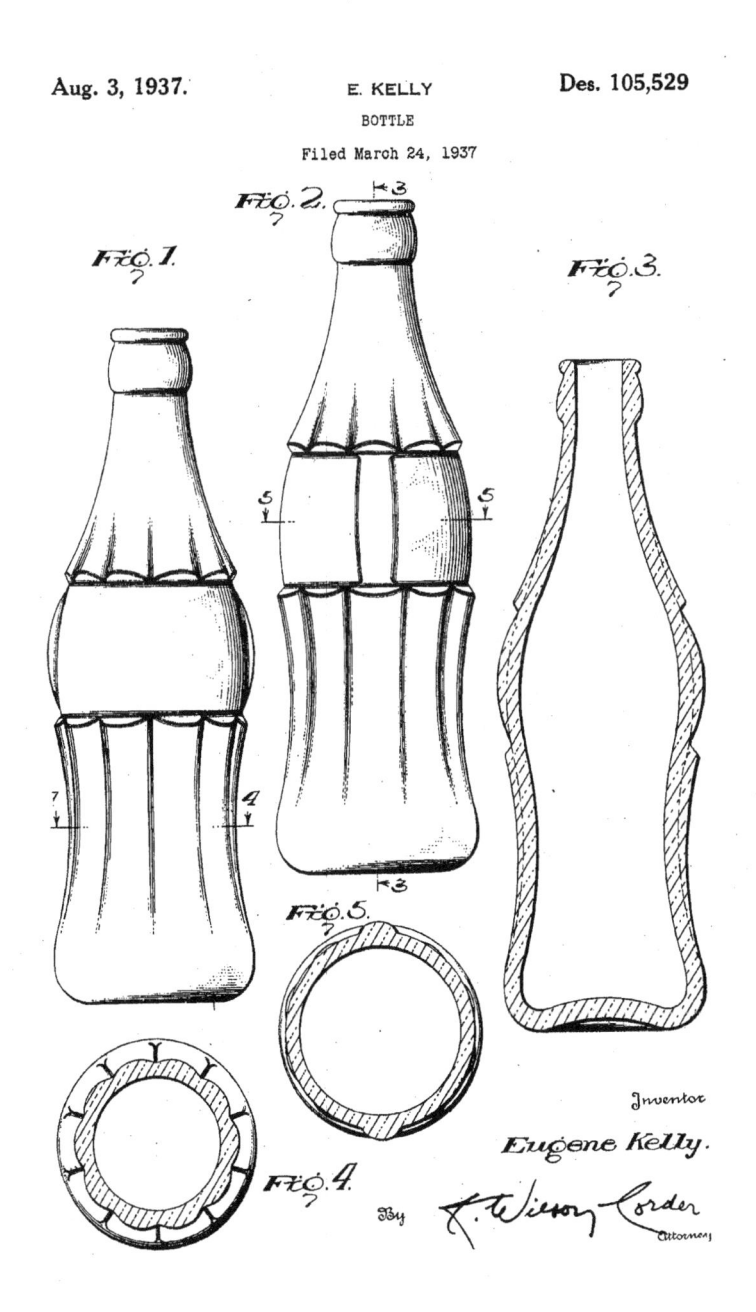

Aug. 3, 1937.   E. KELLY   Des. 105,529
BOTTLE
Filed March 24, 1937

Inventor
Eugene Kelly.
By K. Wilson Corder
Attorney

11

LEGAL BRIEF: INTELLECTUAL PROPERTY

- **Intellectual Property**
  Ideas, inventions, designations, and other intangible creations that provide benefit to their owner.

- **Patent**
  Protects useful and ornamental inventions.

- **Trademark**
  Protects the goodwill of a product or service; used to denote origin of a product traded in commerce.

- **Copyright**
  Protects recorded creative expression; does not protect the idea, only the expression of the idea.

- **Trade Secret**
  Company secret that provides some business advantage to its owner.

CHAPTER TWO

EVERY DISCOVERY EVER MADE

Patents provide temporary monopolies for creators of useful and ornamental inventions. A patent serves as a protection, preventing others from the unauthorized making, using, selling, or offering to sell the invention for a fixed time period—twenty years in the case of utility patents. This protection affords the patent owner the opportunity for economic reward and also serves as an incentive to continue creating other inventions for even further financial gain.

> **Patents exclude others from making, using, selling or offering to sell an invention.**

In exchange for this protection, detailed information regarding the invention is disclosed to the public to be freely used by all, once the patent monopoly expires. In fact, the patent protection is a bargain between the public and the inventor—the almost complete and unfettered protection of temporary exclusivity for an invention in exchange for explicit written instructions on how the invention is made and used.

When examined in specific instances, this bargained exchange is often difficult for many in the public to accept. For example, in the fall of 2001, a terrorist-perpetrated anthrax scare swept the nation, and for a short period of time, the only federally approved treatment was a patented antibiotic called Ciprofloxacin. In order to protect the public from this bioterrorism, the U.S. government sought to place orders for hundreds of millions of doses of this antibiotic, which would have resulted in a tremendous financial windfall for the drug's German manufacturer. Many questioned the appropriateness of allowing a foreign company using a U.S. government-permitted monopoly to charge exorbitant prices to the government in a time of national crisis. Indeed, there was intense pressure from many lawmakers and government watch groups to revoke or suspend the patent for the duration of the crisis. (Canada briefly suspended its patent on this drug shortly after the anthrax threat surfaced.) Fortunately, before this patent issue came to a boiling point, other non-patented drugs were found to be equally effective in treating anthrax infections.

But in the big scheme of incentives and rewards, this bargained exchange, with consideration to the occasional

> The patent monopoly is a bargain between the inventor and the public.

windfall, works extremely well and provides many benefits to the public. Without the potential of large profits, the incentives to take risks in research would be absent. It is true, though, that for the time period an inventor enjoys a monopoly ownership, tremendous hardships may befall the many who cannot afford the inventor's products. However, many more people will benefit from the invention during the term and for the period of usefulness after the patent expires; these people probably wouldn't benefit if the incentives for the product's creation weren't in place.

Patent protection has greatly benefited Priceline.com.

Additionally, in historical terms, twenty years passes relatively quickly. Once the patent term does expire, competition among manufacturers often drives the prices of once expensive, patented goods to a fraction of their original prices.

Because of the significant protection afforded to owners of patents for their inventions, patents are often viewed as exceedingly valuable properties. One of the more breathtaking examples of patent valuation involved the company Priceline.com. Founded in the late 1990s, the company's business model is premised on offering online reverse auctions for travel products such as airline tickets, hotel rooms, and the like. Referred to in the company's advertising as "Name Your Price" purchasing, customers can place a bid for specific products.

For example, you might be interested in flying round-trip from San Francisco to Boston and find that the going rate for coach fare for such a trip is $800. On Priceline.com's website, you can place an irrevocable offer of some lower amount—say $200—for the flight. The airlines having such a flight will look at your bid and decide whether they are interested in accepting your offer at the stated price. In its infancy, Priceline.com received a patent for this online reverse auction process, and although the company was far from being profitable, the company's valuation exceeded $1 billion shortly after the patent was granted.

While it is true that most patents are decidedly not worth $1 billion, patents can be essential to the success of a company. Since resources for start-up companies are limited, almost by definition (except perhaps for that brief period of Internet-related economic insanity that ushered out the last millennium), these

Patent monopolies create barriers to competitors.

The earliest patents were awarded to Italian food recipes.

EVERY DISCOVERY EVER MADE

|||||| |||||||| ||| |||| ||||| |||| |||| |||| ||||| ||||| |||| ||||| ||| |||| |||
US005897620A

United States Patent [19]
Walker et al.

[11] Patent Number: 5,897,620
[45] Date of Patent: Apr. 27, 1999

[54] METHOD AND APPARATUS FOR THE SALE OF AIRLINE-SPECIFIED FLIGHT TICKETS

[75] Inventors: **Jay S. Walker**, Ridgefield; **Thomas M. Sparico**, Riverside; **T. Scott Case**, Darien, all of Conn.

[73] Assignee: priceline.com Inc., Stamford, Conn.

[21] Appl. No.: **08/889,304**
[22] Filed: **Jul. 8, 1997**
[51] Int. Cl.⁶ **G06F 17/60**
[52] U.S. Cl. **705/5**; 705/6
[58] Field of Search 705/5, 6, 7, 9, 705/28; 707/1, 2, 3, 102, 104

[56] **References Cited**

U.S. PATENT DOCUMENTS

4,775,936	10/1988	Jung	705/5
4,845,625	7/1989	Stannard	705/5
4,931,932	6/1990	Dalnekoff et al.	705/5
5,237,499	8/1993	Garback	705/5
5,253,165	10/1993	Leiseca et al.	705/5
5,270,921	12/1993	Hornick	705/6
5,331,546	7/1994	Webber et al.	705/6
5,483,444	1/1996	Heintzeman et al.	705/5
5,570,283	10/1996	Shoolery et al.	705/5
5,797,127	8/1998	Walker et al.	705/5

OTHER PUBLICATIONS

Richard Carroll, *Hitch a Flight to Europe*, p. 1, <http//travelassist.com/mag/a69.html>. not dated.
Airhitch Your Way To Low Cost Travel, pp. 1, 2, <http://www.vaportrails.com/Budget/BudFeatures/Airhitch/Airhitch.html>. not dated.
Sue Goldstein, *Airhitch*, p. 1. not dated.
Miles Poindexter, *Airhitch: Myth or Fact*, pp. 1, 2. not dated.
Frequently Asked Questions about Airhitch, pp. 1–5, 1995, <http://www.isicom.fr/airhitch/ahfaq>.
Across the Atlantic Anytime for $169!!!, pp. 1, 2, <http://www.isicom.fr/airhitch/index.html>. not dated.
Airhitch, General Information, New!!! Target Flights Update, pp. 1–6, <http://www.isicom.fr/airhitch/info.htm>. not dated

Target Flight(R) Quote Request Form, pp. 1, 2, <http://www.isicom.fr/airhitch/tf_qrf.txt>. not dated.
Working For/With Airhitch, pp. 1–5, <http://www.isicom.fr/airhitch/jobs.htm>. not dated.

(List continued on next page.)

Primary Examiner—Stephen R. Tkacs
Attorney, Agent, or Firm—Morgan & Finnegan LLP; Jeffrey L. Brandt

[57] **ABSTRACT**

An unspecified-time airline ticket representing a purchased seat on a flight to be selected later, by the airlines, for a traveler-specified itinerary (e.g., NY to LA on March 3rd) is disclosed. Various methods and systems for matching an unspecified-time ticket with a flight are also disclosed. An exemplary method includes: (1) making available an unspecified-time ticket; (2) examining a plurality of flights which would fulfill the terms of the unspecified-time ticket to determine which flight to select; and (3) providing notification of the selected flight prior to departure. The disclosed embodiments provide travelers with reduced airfare in return for flight-time flexibility and, in turn, permits airlines to fill seats that would have otherwise gone unbooked. Because of the flexibilities required of the unspecified-time traveler, unspecified-time tickets are likely to attract leisure travelers unwilling to purchase tickets at the available published fares and, at the same time, are likely to "fence out" business travelers unwilling to risk losing a full day at either end of their trip. Moreover, the flexibilities required of the unspecified-time traveler need not be limited to a departure time; the flexibilities may also include the airline, the departing airport, the destination airport, or any other restriction that increases the flexibility afforded the airline in placing the traveler aboard a flight. The disclosed embodiments thus permit airlines to fill otherwise empty seats in a manner that stimulates latent and unfulfilled leisure travel demand while leaving their underlying fare structures intact.

101 Claims, 20 Drawing Sheets

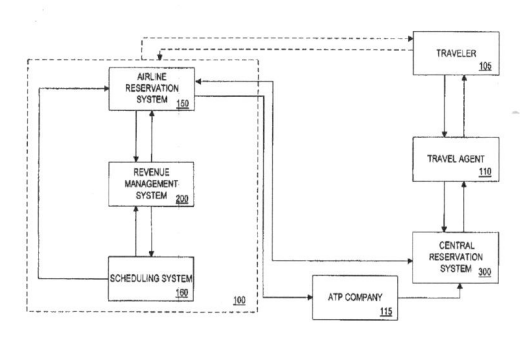

17

new companies are forced to find markets and businesses in which some economic advantage exists. New companies, in particular, cannot out-market and out-spend larger established companies in a fight for market share in markets that have no barriers for entry. Patents provide these barriers for entry. By creating monopolies in critical product-related technologies, companies of all sizes can exclude competitors while building the momentum and market share to reach profitability.

HISTORY OF PATENTS

The American patent system has historical roots in Southern Italy, with the ancient Greek society in Sybaris, as far back as 720 B.C. The Sybarite society, known for its luxurious lifestyle, enacted a law that provided exclusive rights to certain culinary creations. A man who created "any peculiar and excellent dish" was entitled to exclude others from similar creation of that gastronomical delight for a period of one year and was "entitled to all profits to be derived from the manufacture of it for that time." This monopoly of foods was intended to encourage citizens to work and excel at similar creative and beneficial pursuits. While the Sybarite law predates the modern

Fifteenth century Venetian patents lasted for ten years.

American patent system by almost 3,000 years, the similarities between the two are notable in that the creator (inventor) of a new culinary recipe (a new and non-obvious invention) was entitled to the right to exclude others from the production of the same dish for a statutory period of time and entitled to the monetary proceeds from the creation during that time. When that statutory time period reached its end, the populace was enriched by having subsequent use of the new recipe.

The exclusive rights system continued centuries later in Greece, when Hippodamus of Miletus proposed a law that bestowed special honors upon those who made discoveries advantageous to the state, especially as it pertained to architecture and building. Many

Italian inventor Filippo Brunelleschi received early patents for the design of transport vessels.

became critical of this system of exclusivity, and in 480 A.D., the Roman emperor Zeno, outlawed the monopoly system. While Rome was excelling in culture and the arts during this time, however, the empire produced few technological innovations.

Devoid of technological and inventive advancements during the Middle Ages, the incentive and monopoly system returned. Guilds and artisans were granted special rights in an effort to bring the most talented craftsmen and artists to the local community. Monopoly rights were granted in Italy to such prominent individuals as architect and inventor Filippo Brunelleschi for the design of a transport vessel, as well as the textile guilds for designs and patterns. It was in the Venetian Republic in 1474 that the first known patent act was authored. This act provided for "every person who shall build any new and ingenious device...not previously made" to "give notice of it to the office of our General Welfare Board when it has been reduced to perfection so that it can be used and operated." As a part of this revelation to the Welfare Board, it was "forbidden to every other person in any of our territories and towns to make any further device conforming with and similar to said one, without the consent and license of the author, for the term of 10 years." Similar systems eventually were founded in France, Germany, the Netherlands, and England, as the English system formed the basis of the modern American patent system.

During the sixteenth century, England granted a number of monopoly rights. These monopoly rights, most often granted

> Sixteenth century English patents were frequently granted by the Crown as private favors.

to those currying favor with the court, resulted in a public outcry, and the Queen's Bench held that these monopoly grants violated the common law. In 1624, the Bench enacted the Statute of Monopolies that declared these monopolies as void with one exception—the official grant of letters patent. The Statute expressly excluded the prohibition on monopolies to "any letters patent (b) and grants of privilege for the term of fourteen years or under, hereafter to be made, of the sole working or making of any manner of new manufactures within this realm" so long as these grants were not "mischievous to the state." This differed from the previous grant of monopoly rights for political favor.[1]

> The seventeenth century saw reform of the British patent system to eliminate abuse.

More than 200 years later, in 1852, English patent law experienced a significant change that later found its way into U.S. patent law. Whereas previous letters patent were arbitrary grants, this change included a specification to show the scope of the patent. The specification, according to the Bench, allowed for the dissemination of knowledge and indicates one of the underlying concepts of the patent monopoly exchange—exclusive rights in exchange for the contribution of new knowledge to the public.

---

1   Statute of Monopolies 1624, 21 Jac. 1, c. 3, s. 6.

The *quid pro quo* in the 1852 British Patent Act was already present, in part, in the U.S. Constitution, drafted in 1787. Article I, Section 8, Clause 8 of the Constitution held that Congress shall have the power to "promote the Progress of Science and useful Arts by securing for limited Times to Authors and Inventors the exclusive Right to their respective Writings and Discoveries." In exchange for these exclusive rights, the progress of science was furthered by the dissemination of this new knowledge.

The first U.S. patents were issued under the Patent Act of 1790.

The U.S. drafted its first formal Patent Act in 1790 for the issuance of patents for "any useful art, manufacture, engine, machine, or device, or any improvement therein not before known or used."[2] While the act did not create a formal Patent Office, the act did designate a "patent board" that would review applications for letters patent to determine whether an invention was "sufficiently useful and important" as to warrant the grant of a patent. This initial patent board was comprised of the secretary of state, the secretary of war and the attorney general of the U.S. This board issued their first patent to Samuel Hopkins for his method and apparatus of "making Pot ash and Pearl ash." With this review board system, a total of fifty-five

---

2   Patent Act of 1790, ch. 7, § 1, 1 Stat. 109.

patents were granted under the 1790 act.

It did not take long for this three-member board to become overwhelmed, and in 1793, the Patent Act was revised. The 1793 act did away with the review board and examination procedure and instituted a registration system that was clerical. This new system resulted in the registration of countless fraudulent and duplicate patents. Despite the gross shortcomings of this system, it remained in place for almost half-a-century until 1836, when the modern American patent system was born.

Thomas Jefferson was the first patent commissioner.

The 1836 Patent Act brought back the examination process in order to eliminate the duplicity and fraud that existed under the previous act and introduced the non-obviousness requirement, in addition to reintroducing novelty and utility from the initial 1790 act. The 1836 act also created a patent office and a commissioner for patents, as well as a system that allowed for the appeal of adverse examination decisions issued by the patent office. Like the 1852 British Patent Act, a great deal of attention was paid to the scope of the patent and what the inventor sought to claim and bring under the umbrella of the patent grant. The applicant inventor was therefore required to provide a detailed description of his claim in the specification.

The 1836 act survived for more than one hundred years, until it was revamped in 1952, in response to a series of what were considered "anti-patent" decisions by the Supreme Court. The court, over a period of twenty years from the 1930s to the 1950s, had invalidated certain means of drafting patent claims. It also introduced a number of additional requirements for patentability that were not expressly present in the previous patent act, such as *synergism* and the *flash of genius* test.

On September 16, 2011, the America Invents Act (AIA) became law and introduced several major changes to the 1952 act, which would take effect over a period of eighteen months. These changes marked the transition from a first to invent system to a first inventor to file system, the provision of additional options for challenging a granted patent, and the elimination of human organisms and tax strategy methods from patentable subject matter.

U.S. PATENT AND TRADEMARK OFFICE

The business of U.S. patents is handled by the U.S. Patent and Trademark Office (USPTO), an agency of the U.S. Department of Commerce. The role of the USPTO is to examine and grant patents for the protection of inventions and to register trademarks. Apart from its activities in reviewing inventions and granting patents and trademarks, the USPTO indexes and stores all of the detailed invention descriptions of issued patents for use by the public. With more than 8,250,000 patents, this vast storehouse of human knowledge is a technical resource almost beyond comprehension. Virtually every useful discovery or improvement ever made by human beings is described and explained in the files of the USPTO, either as new inventions over the past 300 years or as descriptions of prior art to these newer discoveries. Truly a world treasure, it is the technical center of mankind's universe.

United States Patent and Trademark Office

The USPTO is located in Alexandria, Virginia.

Despite the importance of the USPTO to human innovation, gaining creative insight at this building has historically been like seeking religious enlightenment at the Vatican. It is inspiring to visit, but its size, bureaucracy, and formality make the institution almost unapproachable to the lay person. All this is changing, however, as the power of the Internet has transformed the USPTO into a resource for the masses. Now nearly the entire portfolio of U.S. patents can be searched and retrieved online. Inventors looking for

EVERY DISCOVERY EVER MADE

inspiration—or just inquiring minds—can point their browsers to www.uspto.gov to find a wealth of information. Even the answers to those often puzzling questions asked by inquisitive four-year-olds can be found in the patent files of the USPTO: how do red pimientos get put in the green olives? (U.S. patent 5,100,681); how is spaghetti made? (U.S. patent 6,523,457); and, where do birds go at night? (U.S. patent 4,098,068).

SEARCH patents

Millions of inventions are described at www.uspto.gov.

United States Patent [19]
Masuyama

[11] **4,098,068**
[45] **Jul. 4, 1978**

[54] CUCKOO CLOCK

[76] Inventor: **Isao Masuyama,** 5075, Ohaza Ishioka, Ishioka-shi, Ibaragi-ken, Japan

[21] Appl. No.: **777,406**

[22] Filed: **Mar. 14, 1977**

[30] Foreign Application Priority Data

Mar. 23, 1976 [JP] Japan 51/30810

[51] Int. Cl.² G04B 21/08; G04B 37/00
[52] U.S. Cl. **58/12;** 58/53
[58] Field of Search .... 58/2, 12–14, 58/53–55, 152 R, 152 A, 152 B

[56] References Cited
U.S. PATENT DOCUMENTS

1,041,177	10/1912	Schmidt 58/12
2,054,677	9/1936	Lux 58/12
2,097,818	11/1937	Krakowski 58/16
3,918,249	11/1975	Masuyama 58/12

Primary Examiner—Edith S. Jackmon

[57] **ABSTRACT**

In a cuckoo clock including a timing mechanism and a whistle means for tolling a time, a bird-displaying mechanism comprises- a clock housing having an aperture in the front wall thereof; door means pivotally mounted on the front wall adjacent the aperture; a bird movable into and out of the aperture and having movable wings; plate means pivotally supporting the bird; guiding means having a guiding base slidably supporting the plate means; driving means for driving the guiding means; control means for controlling the driving means in time to a tolling signal from the timing mechanism; spreading means including a rotation lever pivotally mounted on the plate means for spreading the wings when the plate means travels along the guiding base by a predetermined distance in response to the tolling signal.

8 Claims, 8 Drawing Figures

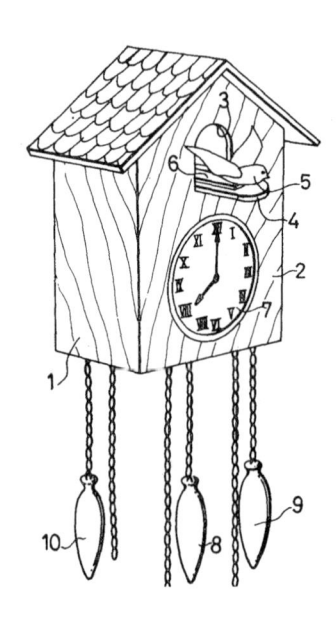

CHAPTER THREE

PATENTS

TYPES OF PATENTS

There are three types of patents that are recognized in the U.S.: utility patents, design patents, and plant patents. Utility patents protect systems and methods, apparatuses, structures, and compounds; design patents protect novel designs; and plant patents protect asexually reproducing plants.

Nearly 500,000 U.S. patent applications are filed each year.

UTILITY PATENTS

Utility patents are the broad machine and process patent grants that we often think of when considering invention protection; these are the workhorses of intellectual property protection. Utility patents protect the structure and functionality of a product—how the product works, how it is made, and how it is used.

Although utility patents are expensive and time-consuming

PATENTS

Design patents are valid for fourteen years from the issue date.

to secure, the protection afforded a patented invention can be quite broad and difficult to challenge. Utility patents are usually issued from two to three years after the filing of a patent application and are valid for twenty years from the date of the filing.

DESIGN PATENTS

Design patents protect ornamental features of an invention. A tremendous amount of effort and engineering often goes into the aesthetic development of a commercial product. Whether the product is a toothpaste container or a kitchen appliance, hundreds of hours are often spent modeling and prototyping the look and feel of the product.

For instance, the Polycom SoundStation®—the ubiquitous, triangular-shaped speakerphone found in the vast majority of conference rooms in the U.S.—is protected by a design patent issued in 1993. Design patents generally cost about one-fifth of the price of a utility patent, issue in less than one year from filing, and are valid for fourteen years from the date of issue. Because of their relatively low cost and speedy issuance, design patents are an excellent intellectual property protection value.

PLANT PATENTS

The U.S. patent laws also provide for the protection of new and distinct varieties of asexually reproducing plants, otherwise known as plant patents. Like utility patents, they are valid for twenty years from the date of filing, but the published patents are usually quite notable because of the beautifully colored photographs that frequently accompany the applications.

Plant patents afford the owner the same exclusive rights as any other patent, but a critical element to note is that the plant must be asexual, which means that the plants must make exact copies of themselves when they go through reproduction. Other federal statutes protect sexually reproducing plants, providing broad protection for those involved in agriculture research and development.

PROVISIONAL PATENT APPLICATIONS

In addition to the regular patent application procedure described above, it is possible to file what is called a provisional patent application. This type of patent application is similar in many respects to the regular patent application, except that the provisional

Provisional patent applications expire after one year.

United States Patent [19]
Hinman et al.

[11] Patent Number: **Des. 342,732**
[45] Date of Patent: ∗∗ Dec. 28, 1993

[54] **SPEAKER PHONE**

[75] Inventors: Brian Hinman, Los Gatos, Calif.; Scott Wakefield, Andover, Mass.

[73] Assignee: Polycom, Inc., San Jose, Calif.

[∗∗] Term: **14 Years**

[21] Appl. No.: **903,543**

[22] Filed: **Jun. 23, 1992**
[52] U.S. Cl. D14/150
[58] Field of Search D14/140, 142, 149, 150, D14/240, 243, 188, 189, 217, 218; 379/202, 419, 440, 428, 434

[56] **References Cited**
U.S. PATENT DOCUMENTS

D. 292,283 10/1987 Matsuda D14/240
D. 300,322   3/1989 Iam D14/189
D. 325,734   4/1992 Miyai D14/189
D. 331,060 11/1992 Emmons et al. D14/218

Primary Examiner—Alan P. Douglas
Assistant Examiner—Jeffrey Asch
Attorney, Agent, or Firm—John S. Ferrell

[57] **CLAIM**

The ornamental design of the speaker phone, as described and shown.

DESCRIPTION

FIG. 1 is a perspective of the speaker phone showing our new design;
FIG. 2 is a top view of the speaker phone;
FIG. 3 is a front view of the speaker phone;
FIG. 4 is a side view of the speaker phone the opposite side being a mirror image thereof;
FIG. 5 is a back view of the speaker phone; and,
FIG. 6 is a bottom view of the speaker phone.
The circular apertures schematically depicted in the circular feature at the top in FIGS. 1-5 are continuous throughout.

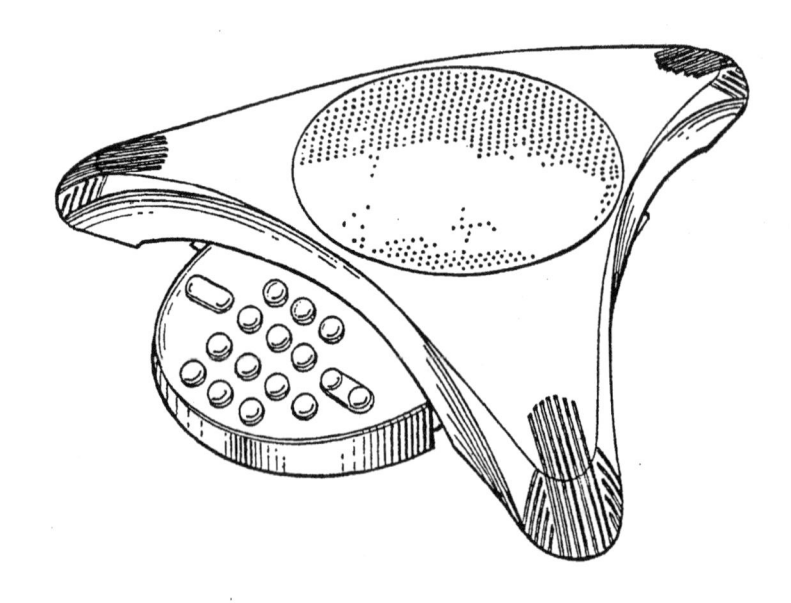

PATENTS

A Polycom SoundStation®—the ubiquitous, triangular-shaped speakerphone found in conference rooms throughout the U.S.

# United States Patent [19]
Zary

[11] Patent Number: Plant 11,691
[45] Date of Patent: Dec. 12, 2000

[54] HYBRID TEA ROSE PLANT NAMED 'JACNEPAL'

[75] Inventor: Keith W. Zary, Thousand Oaks, Calif.

[73] Assignee: Bear Creek Gardens, Inc., Medford, Oreg.

[21] Appl. No.: 09/255,437

[22] Filed: Feb. 22, 1999

[51] Int. Cl.⁷ A01H 5/00
[52] U.S. Cl. Plt./132
[58] Field of Search Plt./132, 130

Primary Examiner—Howard J. Locker
Attorney, Agent, or Firm—Klarquist Sparkman Campbell Leigh & Whinston, LLP

[57] ABSTRACT

A hybrid tea rose plant having vigorous, upright growth; large flowers produced one per stem; mildew and rust resistant foliage; a blend of colors in the flower; and stems long enough for cutting.

1 Drawing Sheet

The present invention relates to a new and distinct variety of rose plant of the hybrid tea class which was originated by me by crossing JACyap (not patented), with MACnewye (U.S. Plant Pat. No. 5,428).

The primary objective of this breeding was to produce a new rose variety having vigorous, upright growth; large flowers produced one per stem; disease resistant foliage; a blend of colors in the flower; and stems long enough for cutting. The objective was substantially achieved, along with other desirable improvements, as evidenced by the following unique combination of characteristics that are otustanding in the new variety and that distinguish it from its parents, as well as from all other varieties of which I am aware:

1. High centered large flowers;
2. Long stems;
3. Blooms one flower per stem;
4. Dark green, glossy, disease resistant foliage;
5. Vigorous, upright growing plant;
6. Flowers that exhibit a blend of colors.

JACnepal is a vigorous, upright, well-branched garden hybrid tea. It produces long-stemmed, large-flowered roses that are a bend of colors. Foliage is dark green, glossy, and very disease resistant.

Asexual reproduction of this new variety by budding, as performed at Wasco, Calif., shows that the foregoing and all other characteristics and distinctions come true to form and are established and transmitted through succeeding propagations.

The accompanying illustration shows typical specimens of the vegetative growth and flowers of this new variety in different stages of development, depicted in color as nearly true as it is reasonably possible to make the same in a color illustration of this character.

The following is a detailed description of my new rose cultivar with color descriptions using terminology in accordance with The Royal Horticultural Society (London) Colour Chart, except where ordinary dictionary significance of color is indicted.

Parentage:
 Seed parent.—JACyap (not patented).
 Pollen parent.—MACnewye (U.S. Plant Pat. No. 5,428).
Classification:
 Botanical.—Rosa hybrida.
 Commercial.—Hybrid tea.

FLOWER

Observations made from specimens grown in a garden environment at Somis, Calif. January 1996–December 1998.

Blooming habit: Continuous.
Bud:
 Size.—1¾ inches long when the petals start to unfurl.
 Form.—The bud form is long, pointed ovoid.
 Color.—When sepals first divide, the bud color is Orange-White Group 159D with petal edges and tips Red Group 45D. When half blown, the upper sides of the petals are Orange-White Group 159D with petal edges Red Group 45D, and the lower sides of the petals are Orange-White Group 159D with petal edges Red Group 45D.
 Sepals.—Color: Green Group 138B except when exposed to direct sunlight. Then, sepals are blushed with Greyed-Purple Group 183D. Surface texture: Covered in fine hairs. There are three normally appendaged sepals. There are two unappendaged sepals with hair edges.
 Receptacle.—Color: Green Group 137D except when exposed to bright sunlight. Then the color is Greyed-Purple Group 183C. Shape: Funnel. Size: Large (⁷⁄₁₆" long×⅝" wide). Surface: Smooth.
 Peduncle.—Length: Short (averaging 2½ to 3"). Surface: Glandular. Color: Green Group 137D except when exposed to bright sunlight. Then the color is Greyed-Purple Group 183C. Strength: Stiff; erect.
Bloom:
 Size.—Large. Average open size is 5 to 5½".
 Borne.—Singly.
 Stems.—Strength: Strong. Average length is 16–20".
 Form.—When first open: High centered. Permanence: Retains its form to the end. Outer petals curl back.
 Petalage.—Number of petals under normal conditions: 30–35.
 Color.—The upper sides of the petals are Orange-White Group 159D with petal edges Red Group 45D. The reverse sides of the petals are Orange-White Group 159D with petal edges Red Group 45D. The base of each petal has on both surfaces a ¼×¼" Yellow Group 12B half moon at the point of attachment. The major color on the upper sides is Orange-White Group 159D.
 Variegations.—None.
 Discoloration.—At the end of the first day: No change. At the end of the third day: No change. By day five or six, on the plant, there is a fading of color on the petal edges to Red Group 48B.
 Fragrance.—Moderate; spicy.

application is never examined by the USPTO. The provisional patent application acts as a priority date placeholder and may be replaced by a regular non-provisional utility, design or plant patent application within one year of the provisional application's filing date.

The use of provisional applications in the U.S. was first

Plant patents often contain beautiful color photographs.

allowed in 1994. Thus, provisional applications are relatively new, and some controversy exists among patent professionals as to whether or not these placeholder applications are advantageous for inventors.

> **Patent applications must teach all elements necessary to practice the invention.**

A provisional application allows the establishment of an early priority date for the purposes of filing patents in foreign countries and lowers the formality requirements since the provisional applications are not examined. For these applications, drawings can be hand-sketched, perfect grammar is not essential, and no patent claims are required. With lessened formality requirements, the cost of preparation could, in theory, be somewhat less, thus allowing the inventor one year to test the invention before fully committing to the cost of a regular patent application.

It is important to note, however, that the requirement for clearly and fully explaining the invention is the same for the provisional application as it is for the non-provisional. By using the provisional application as a low-cost, temporary alternative to a non-provisional patent filing, inventors may run the risk of taking shortcuts in their provisional applications, which might jeopardize their non-provisional applications later.

Given the reduced formality requirements and the early

priority date, provisional applications may be useful in several situations. One example would be to protect the inventor's rights before displaying the invention at a trade show. Another would be the year to consider the merits of the invention, during which the inventor may seek a licensee or additional funding to develop the product.

If the provisional application route is used, the inventor should ask, "Could someone of ordinary skill in the art—who is reading this description—practice the invention described?" Another consideration that must be made when filing a provisional application is whether the inventor has explained the best mode of practicing the invention. Unlike secret family recipes, which, when casually shared, might be missing a vital ingredient or two, patent applicants are duty-bound to teach the world all of the details of the best embodiment they know. However, leaving the secret sauce out of your patent application will no longer result in an invalid patent or claim in the event of a lawsuit. To be safe, provisional applications must contain all of the invention details also.

WHAT CAN BE PATENTED?

Nearly anything can be patented. Machines, medicines, computer programs, articles made by machines, compositions, chemicals, biogenetic material, and processes, can all be the subject matter for a U.S. patent. To get some handle on the contours of patentability, it is sometimes easier to think of the things that cannot be patented.

Inventions that are inoperative cannot be patented. The USPTO defines *inoperative* to mean that the invention does not produce the claimed results by the applicant. These inventions can usually be identified through their "incredible" utility. For example, in 1979, Joseph Newman attempted to patent a motor with one hundred percent efficiency, i.e., a perpetual motion machine. Such a machine was thought to be "incredible" because it would violate the laws of physics. Several tests showed that Newman's device did not operate with one hundred percent efficiency and thus was considered inoperative. Other examples of inoperative inventions include cold fusion and uncharacterized

Although many have tried, no perpetual motion machines have ever been patented.

PATENTS

(12) United States Patent
Armstrong

(10) Patent No.: US 6,293,874 B1
(45) Date of Patent: Sep. 25, 2001

(54) **USER-OPERATED AMUSEMENT APPARATUS FOR KICKING THE USER'S BUTTOCKS**

(76) Inventor: **Joe W. Armstrong**, 306 Kingston St., Lenoir, TN (US) 37771-2408

(*) Notice: Subject to any disclaimer, the term of this patent is extended or adjusted under 35 U.S.C. 154(b) by 0 days.

(21) Appl. No.: **09/477,175**

(22) Filed: **Jan. 4, 2000**

(51) Int. Cl.[7] **A63H 37/00**
(52) U.S. Cl. **472/51; 472/55**
(58) Field of Search 472/51, 55, 137; 482/51, 72, 148

(56) **References Cited**

U.S. PATENT DOCUMENTS

654,611	7/1900	De Moulin .
920,837	5/1909	De Moulin .
953,411	3/1910	De Moulin .
966,935	8/1910	Mamaux .
976,851	11/1910	De Moulin .
1,175,372	3/1916	Newcomb .
4,457,100	* 7/1984	Nightingale 446/333
5,785,601	* 7/1998	Kubcshcski et al. 472/135

* cited by examiner

Primary Examiner—Joe H. Cheng
Assistant Examiner—Kim T. Nguyen
(74) *Attorney, Agent, or Firm*—Pitts & Brittian, P.C.

(57) **ABSTRACT**

An amusement apparatus including a user-operated and controlled apparatus for self-infliction of repetitive blows to the user's buttocks by a plurality of elongated arms bearing flexible extensions that rotate under the user's control. The apparatus includes a platform foldable at a mid-section, having first post and second upstanding posts detachably mounted thereon. The first post is provided with a crank positioned at a height thereon which requires the user to bend forward toward the first post while grasping the crank with both hands, to prominently present his buttocks toward the second post. The second post is provided with a plurality of rotating arms detachably mounted thereon, with a central axis of the rotating arms positioned at a height generally level with the user's buttocks. The elongated arms are propelled by the user's movement of the crank, which is operatively connected by a drive train to the central axis of the rotating arms. As the user rotates the crank, the user's buttocks are paddled by flexible shoes located on each outboard end of the elongated arms to provide amusement to the user and viewers of the paddling. The amusement apparatus is foldable into a self-contained package for storage or shipping.

14 Claims, 7 Drawing Sheets

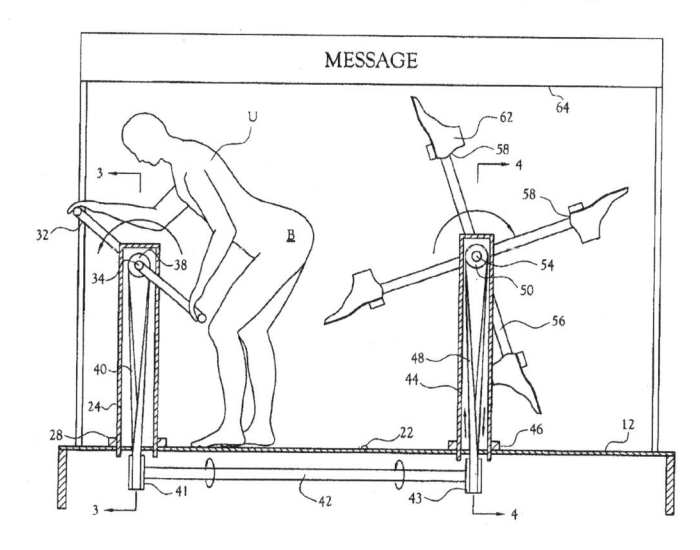

PATENTS

(12) United States Patent
Olson

(10) Patent No.: **US 6,368,227 B1**
(45) Date of Patent: **Apr. 9, 2002**

(54) **METHOD OF SWINGING ON A SWING**

(76) Inventor: **Steven Olson**, 337 Otis Ave., St. Paul, MN (US) 55104

(*) Notice: Subject to any disclaimer, the term of this patent is extended or adjusted under 35 U.S.C. 154(b) by 0 days.

(21) Appl. No.: **09/715,198**

(22) Filed: **Nov. 17, 2000**

(51) Int. Cl.[7] A63G 9/00
(52) U.S. Cl. 472/118
(58) Field of Search 472/118, 119, 472/120, 121, 122, 123, 125

(56) **References Cited**

U.S. PATENT DOCUMENTS

242,601 A * 6/1881 Clement 472/118

5,413,298 A * 5/1995 Perreault 248/228

* cited by examiner

Primary Examiner—Kien T. Nguyen
(74) *Attorney, Agent, or Firm*—Peter Lowell Olson

(57) **ABSTRACT**

A method of swing on a swing is disclosed, in which a user positioned on a standard swing suspended by two chains from a substantially horizontal tree branch induces side to side motion by pulling alternately on one chain and then the other.

4 Claims, 3 Drawing Sheets

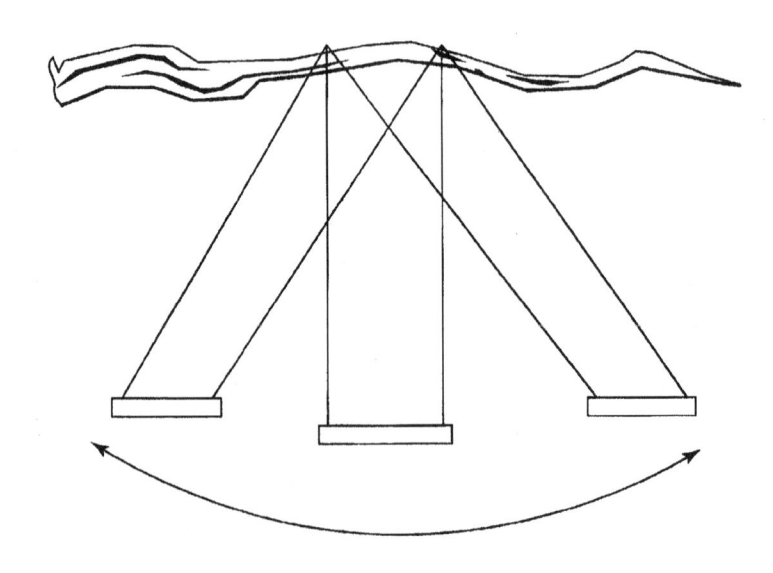

40

United States Patent [19]
Cohen

[11] Patent Number: 5,356,330
[45] Date of Patent: Oct. 18, 1994

[54] APPARATUS FOR SIMULATING A "HIGH FIVE"

[76] Inventor: Albert Cohen, 176 N. Lake Ave., Troy, N.Y. 12180

[21] Appl. No.: 163,856

[22] Filed: Dec. 7, 1993

[51] Int. Cl.[5] A63H 33/00; A63H 3/36
[52] U.S. Cl. 446/491; 446/390; 472/70
[58] Field of Search 446/390, 485, 491; 40/418, 490; 472/70; 482/83, 84, 85, 86

[56] References Cited
U.S. PATENT DOCUMENTS

1,425,945	8/1922	Congdon .
2,484,343	10/1949	Hawes .
2,585,780	2/1952	Johnson .
2,937,872	5/1960	Gilman .
3,252,242	5/1966	Zalkind .
3,427,021	2/1969	Donato 482/83
3,755,960	9/1973	Tepper et al. 446/299
3,804,406	4/1974	Viscione .... 482/83 X
3,877,697	4/1975	Lersch .
3,927,879	12/1975	Long et al. 482/83
4,381,620	5/1983	Panzarella .
5,171,197	12/1992	Healy et al. 482/83

FOREIGN PATENT DOCUMENTS

563984 7/1977 U.S.S.R. 482/83

Primary Examiner—Robert A. Hafer
Assistant Examiner—D. Neal Muir
Attorney, Agent, or Firm—Schmeiser, Morelle & Watts

[57] ABSTRACT

An apparatus for simulating a "high-five" including a lower arm portion having a simulated hand removably attached thereto, an upper arm portion, an elbow joint for pivotally securing the lower arm portion to the upper arm portion, and a spring biasing element for biasing the upper and lower arm portions towards a predetermined alignment.

12 Claims, 3 Drawing Sheets

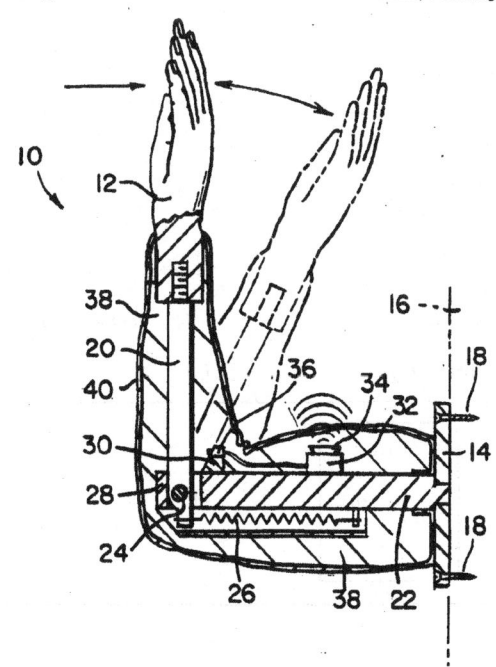

PATENTS

US006086697A

United States Patent [19]
Key

[11] Patent Number: 6,086,697
[45] Date of Patent: Jul. 11, 2000

[54] ROTATING LABEL SYSTEM AND METHOD

[75] Inventor: **Stephen M. Key**, Oakdale, Calif.

[73] Assignee: **Stephen Key Design, LLC**, Oakdale, Calif.

[21] Appl. No.: **09/126,010**

[22] Filed: **Jul. 29, 1998**

[51] Int. Cl.[7] **B65C 3/08**; G09F 3/00
[52] U.S. Cl. **156/215**; 156/DIG. 9; 40/306; 40/310; 40/506; 428/43; 428/343
[58] Field of Search .... 156/212, 213, 156/215, 447, 475, DIG. 9, DIG. 10, DIG. 11, DIG. 12, DIG. 13, DIG. 18, DIG. 26, DIG. 34; 40/306, 310, 506; 428/41.7, 41.8, 43, 343

[56] **References Cited**

U.S. PATENT DOCUMENTS

736,035	8/1903	Stevenson .
1,064,576	6/1913	Washburn .
1,312,611	8/1919	Chess .
1,334,031	3/1920	Hahn 40/335
1,387,625	8/1921	Stein 1/95
1,486,313	3/1924	Van Antwerp .
2,013,616	9/1935	Rettemeyer 220/1
2,129,364	9/1938	Simons et al. 283/8
2,441,607	5/1948	Walls 46/13
2,468,000	4/1949	Taylor 273/143
2,504,076	4/1950	Lindblom 40/68
2,844,893	7/1958	Keller 40/4
2,860,431	11/1958	Barnum 40/61
2,931,657	4/1960	Lewis 273/155
2,935,814	5/1960	Freeze 46/36
2,971,283	2/1961	Parker 40/334
3,278,182	10/1966	Lescher 272/8
3,374,911	3/1968	White 215/8
3,488,880	1/1970	Taylor 46/24
3,542,229	11/1970	Beyerlein et al. 215/1
3,604,584	9/1971	Shank .... 215/12 R
3,733,002	5/1973	Fujio .... 215/12 R
3,960,713	6/1976	Carey 206/534
4,044,889	8/1977	Orentreich 206/459
4,057,251	11/1977	Jones et al. .... 273/95 R
4,203,240	5/1980	Goodwin 40/310
4,312,523	1/1982	Haines .... 40/306 X
4,381,615	5/1983	Lonsmin 40/334
4,405,045	9/1983	Villa-Real 206/534
4,505,497	3/1985	Katzman 283/81
4,567,681	2/1986	Fumei 40/310
4,658,974	4/1987	Fujita et al. .... 215/12 R
4,724,973	2/1988	Shah 215/246
4,844,760	7/1989	Dickey 156/215
4,877,119	10/1989	Hosking 206/459
5,076,613	12/1991	Kovacs 283/106
5,116,452	5/1992	Eder 156/566
5,154,448	10/1992	Griffin et al. 283/102
5,321,933	6/1994	Seifert et al. 53/415
5,324,559	6/1994	Brombacher 428/40
5,342,093	8/1994	Weernink 285/81
5,403,636	4/1995	Crum 428/40
5,639,529	6/1997	Gozdecki et al. .... 40/310 X
5,800,893	9/1998	Harden .... 428/41.7 X
5,809,674	9/1998	Key 40/306
5,884,421	3/1999	Key 40/306
5,953,170	9/1999	Glancy .... 40/310 X

FOREIGN PATENT DOCUMENTS

85214	3/1958	Denmark .
965522	9/1950	France .
1347102	11/1963	France .
2460260	1/1981	France .
285514	10/1988	France .
2677786	12/1992	France .
1565	6/1888	Sweden .

Primary Examiner—Curtis Mayes
Attorney, Agent, or Firm—Carr & Ferrell LLP

[57] **ABSTRACT**

A system and method are disclosed for constructing a rotatable label and attaching the rotatable label to a container. The rotatable label includes a release tab releasably attached to an outer label. The release tab is adhered to the container, or to an inner label adhered to the container, to secure the outer label to the container while the outer label is wrapped around the container. The release tab may then be detached from the outer label to permit the outer label to be rotated about the container. Longitudinal movement of the outer label relative to the container may be restricted by disposing the outer label between top and bottom label panels formed on the container. The outer label is preferably adapted with a transparent portion or window permitting viewing of indicia disposed therebehind.

34 Claims, 9 Drawing Sheets

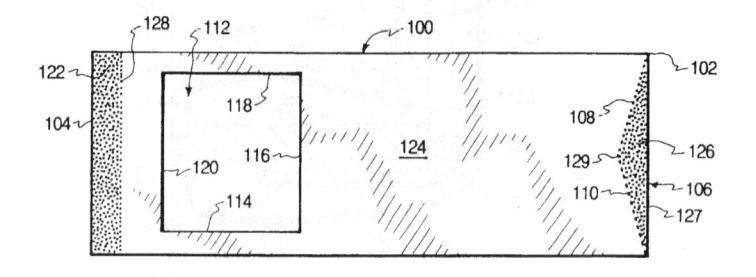

42

United States Patent [19]
Cane

[11] Patent Number: **5,523,741**
[45] Date of Patent: **Jun. 4, 1996**

[54] SANTA CLAUS DETECTOR

[76] Inventor: Thomas Cane, 28 Westwood Dr., San Rafael, Calif. 94901

[21] Appl. No.: **293,673**

[22] Filed: **Aug. 19, 1994**

[51] Int. Cl.[6] G08B 23/00
[52] U.S. Cl. 340/573; 362/103; 362/801; 362/802; 362/806; 36/137
[58] Field of Search 340/573; 36/137; 362/103, 801, 802, 806, 808

[56] References Cited

U.S. PATENT DOCUMENTS

3,220,130	11/1965	Falkenberg	362/808
3,525,862	8/1970	Carter	362/808
4,823,240	4/1989	Shenker	362/808
4,833,580	5/1989	Allen	362/806
4,858,079	8/1989	Ohashi	362/806
5,033,212	7/1991	Evanyk	36/137
5,361,192	11/1994	Lai	362/806

Primary Examiner—Brent A. Swarthout
Assistant Examiner—Albert K. Wong
Attorney, Agent, or Firm—Ralph C. Francis

[57] **ABSTRACT**

A children's Christmas Stocking device useful for visually signalling the arrival of Santa Claus by illuminating an externally visable light source having a power source located within said device.

4 Claims, 4 Drawing Sheets

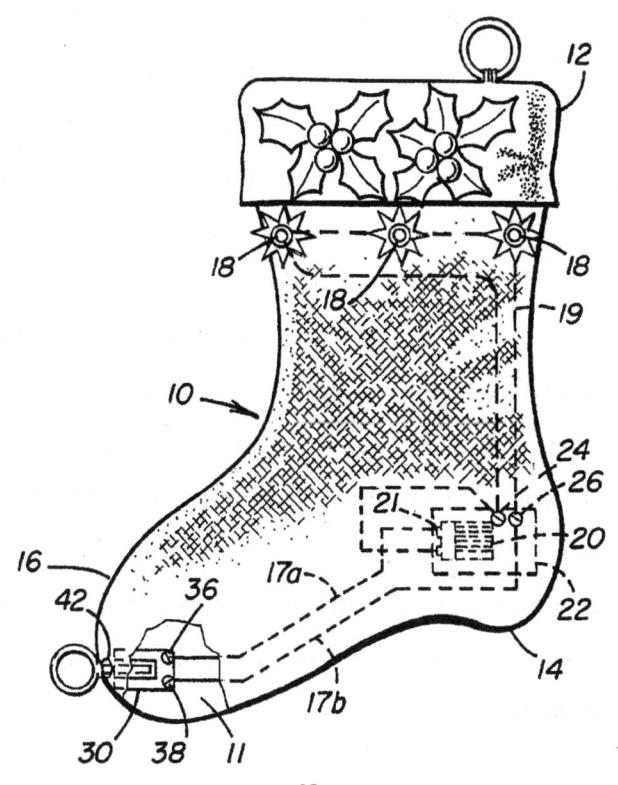

PATENTS

compositions for curing a wide array of cancers.

Laws of nature also cannot be patented. Had Sir Isaac Newton been struck by a falling apple anywhere in America, whether that be in northern Georgia or central Washington state, his discovery of gravity would not have been the proper subject matter for a U.S. patent application. Gravity is a law of nature, as is entropy, the theory of general relativity, sunshine, and the vagaries of weather.

Materials for atomic weapons cannot be patented, presumably because the USPTO is happy not to have the recipe for these materials available for public consumption.

Articles contrary to the public good are not patentable. Since assisting suicide is a crime in all of the U.S., machines that are dedicated to enabling suicide would not be patentable. Additionally, methods of reducing, avoiding, or deferring tax liability are no longer patentable because it would not be fair to prevent other taxpayers from implementing an interpretation of the tax code.

Patents often enable product monopolies and allow inventors to control markets.

Also, human organisms are not patentable because the government does not want to give someone a monopoly on human beings.

PATENTS

Aside from these few categories, virtually anything that is new, useful, and non-obvious can be patented. To fully appreciate the bizarre range of inventions accepted by the USPTO, visit the online patent database at www.uspto.gov.

WHY DO PATENTS MATTER?

Patents are critically important to many kinds of businesses, particularly businesses that rely on technology and innovation for effectively competing with others in their industry. The evolution of products in these types of industries tends to be so rapid and perpetual, it can be quite challenging just to keep up with the momentous progression, much less protect the ingenuity in a timely manner along the way. But, the procurement of the protection a patent offers can provide businesses with five major benefits.

Patents should be viewed as business tools, not technology awards.

First and foremost, *patents may enable limited monopolies for their owners*. These monopolies often allow a company a quiet period of up to two decades to reap the exclusive benefits of resources invested in research and product development.

A second benefit of patents indicates *patents protect the invention from unexpectedly leaving the business*. Like a ball and chain tethered to the technology, the patent prevents ex-employees, customers, and competitors from taking the innovation and marketing their own competing products.

Third, *patents provide a tangible measure of research and product development output.* Patents allow companies to keep score of how effectively their research efforts are producing innovative ideas, and provide an excellent way of memorializing and organizing these inventions.

Fourth, *patents provide any business in a competitive industry a defensive bargaining chip to exchange in the event that the business finds itself the target of someone else's patent.* Since patent owners may completely exclude others from practicing their inventions, the mere payment of money to a patent owner may not be sufficient enough to enable an infringer to stay in business. Often, the threat of a patent counterclaim and the resulting exchange of patent rights is the only way that aggressive competitors can coexist. Without patents, operating a technology business in a crowded market is akin to swimming in a shark tank with a nosebleed.

File patents on important product features.

Finally, *patents allow sophisticated entrepreneurs and businesses to exercise control over their markets.* With well-planned patent filings, a company may be able to control its own destiny and greatly impact the futures of its competitors. This process, called strategic patenting, looks at a company's product plans as well as the product roadmaps and patent portfolios of key competitors. To examine a company's product plans, initial questions asked in this process may include:

- "What are the key technologies needed to extend current products into the future?"
- "How can we control these technologies and prevent others from hijacking our roadmap?"
- "Where can we find missing technologies needed to extend the product plan?"

APPLYING FOR PATENTS

The patent application process begins with identifying the invention. An invention, for purposes of patent protection, must be new, useful, and non-obvious.

Patentable inventions do not need to be Nobel Prize candidates; they merely need to have some modest amount of utility. From a practical perspective, resources should not be wasted on seeking patents of little or no commercial value. You may recall that patents grant the right to exclude others from practicing an invention. If there is no commercial value to an invention, the patent is wasted since there may not be any competitors to exclude.

Avoid wasting resources on patenting "stealth inventions."

PATENTS

When trying to decide what to patent, a useful step is to observe the features in the product that would make customers want to purchase it. Ask the question: "What differentiates our product from similar products manufactured and sold by others?" It is these differentiating features that should be considered for patent protection. Patents for technologies that are buried deep within a product also called "stealth inventions" are often not useful, since it may be impossible to determine whether anyone is actually infringing upon the patent. For the patent to be valuable, it should not only cover features that provide a business advantage or distinguish a product from a competitor's product but also cover features with characteristics that are detectable by the patent owner. It is important to be able to determine relatively easily if a competitor's product utilizes the patented technology and thus infringes the patent.

For example, a computer program may execute a series of incredibly efficient calculations that produces some result. Although this calculation may be extremely novel and unique, having a patent on this calculation would not be useful if it was impossible to determine if the computer was actually implementing the calculation. Although it is true that the patent owner would have the right to exclude others from practicing this stealth invention, it might be impossible or extremely difficult for him to ever know if an actual infringement was occurring. On the other hand, if a specific display—that only could have been produced as a result of the calculation—was produced on the computer screen, then patenting the calculation would be useful. In this case, it would be possible on simple inspection to know by virtue of the display if the calculation was being infringed upon. Therefore, an important aspect of deciding what to patent is the feasibility of detecting whether or not others are infringing upon the patent.

Once the patentable invention is identified, it is important to isolate the inventive feature(s). The inventive feature is often called the "point of novelty" of the invention. It is this point of novelty that will form the basis for the patent application.

Patent applications are published by the USPTO eighteen months after the original filing.

The patent application consists of a set of figures or drawings, a detailed description of the invention, and a set of patent claims that very precisely sets forth the scope and contours of the invention. The normal process of preparing and filing a patent application includes a meeting with an attorney or registered patent agent to discuss the invention and to identify the point of novelty. Following this meeting, the attorney may take several weeks to draft the patent application, after which the inventor reviews and edits the application in

PATENTS

preparation for filing. Once the patent application is filed with the USPTO, approximately eighteen to thirty months will pass, during which time the examiner at the USPTO will review the application and search other patents and related publications to determine if the invention is novel. After the search and examination processes are complete, the patent examiner will return comments to the inventor's attorney or agent in the form of an office action. The attorney or agent usually is requested to provide arguments distinguishing the filed patent claims from prior patents and publications that were identified during the search. On average, a patent application requires between two and three years to mature from an initial filing to an issued patent grant. After a total of about three years, a U.S. utility patent is issued and remains valid for a period of twenty years following the initial filing date of the patent. In order to keep the patent enforceable following issuance, the inventor is required to pay maintenance fees to the USPTO every four years.

> Once filed, patents often take two to three years to issue.

> Utility patents are valid for up to twenty years from the date of filing.

The cost of preparing and filing a patent application can

vary dramatically, based on such factors as the technology of the invention, the skill and experience of the attorney or agent preparing the application, and the involvement of the inventor in the process. Simple mechanical patent applications in many cases can be prepared for less than $10,000, while some drug-related applications might exceed $40,000 to prepare and file. After the patent application is filed, likely an additional $5,000 to $15,000 or more will be spent responding to the USPTO and amending the application for allowance, prior to issuance. Several more thousands of dollars will be spent on the issue fee and maintenance fees over the twenty-year life of the patent.

Although patents can be incredibly valuable, they are not inexpensive. Whether a do-it-yourself application or one prepared by a premier patent firm, a patent can make expensive wallpaper if not reserved for commercially viable inventions. Before committing the time and money to the patent process, consider carefully whether the prospective economic return exists to justify the investment.

LEGAL BRIEF: TYPES OF PATENTS

- **Utility Patent**
  Protects new, useful, and non-obvious inventions; common inventions include machines, processes, chemical compounds, and articles of manufacture.

- **Design Patent**
  Protects new, ornamental, and non-obvious designs, particularly industrial designs of products.

- **Plant Patent**
  Protects asexually reproducing plants.

■ CHAPTER FOUR ■

TRADEMARKS

Trademarks identify the source or manufacturer of a product or service. Nearly any word, name, symbol, or device used in commerce in connection with a product or service may be used as a trademark. While this protection is not absolute, it does act, and hopefully help, to prevent conflicting words, names, or symbols from being confused with similar products or services in the same geographic region. (An example of trademark confusion might be represented by the satirical Jack in the Box commercials of several years ago, in which Jack confuses the fast food restaurant, Wendy's, with a house of a woman named Wendy.)

Trademarks protect the goodwill of a product's source or manufacturer.

Many kinds of symbols can be used as trademarks. Not only are there trade names (the name a company does business under) and company logos that can be registered as trademarks (such as Wendy's and the NBC peacock), but sounds can be registered trademarks, too. For instance, who can listen to the middle passages of George Gershwin's *Rhapsody in Blue* without thinking

TRADEMARKS

of United Airlines, or the distinctive roar of the MGM lion without knowing its source? Trademarks are also available for colors and smells, as in the color pink with Owens-Corning Fiberglas® insulation and scented yarn. Product shapes (the original Coke bottle), packaging, the look and feel of a business establishment (Fuddruckers, Inc.), and even sales techniques all have the capability of being trademarked.

The ® symbol designates that the trademark has been registered with the USPTO.

All of these versions of trademarks can be registered with the USPTO, providing many statutory benefits. First, the act of registration puts the entire world on notice regarding the ownership of the trademark. This notice also serves to prevent any second-party claims from so-called innocent infringers who may attempt to use a mark on a similar good or service and then claim to be unaware of its ownership. To further punctuate this notice to the marketplace, the right to display the ® symbol is also granted.

However, trademark protection might still exist, even if the mark or symbol is never registered. It's very common for trademark rights to be acquired through common law, under which trademark rights begin to accrue when a mark is used consistently to identify the source of a product or service. The common law rights also apply to trade dress or the look and feel of a product or business. For example, Taco Cabana, a fast-food Mexican restaurant, opened its first restaurant in San Antonio, Texas, in 1978. The restaurant had a distinctive color scheme with bright awnings and a patio café concept. Two Pesos opened competing restaurants in 1985 with a similar motif, and was later found to have deliberately infringed Taco Cabana's trade dress. However, certain elements must be in place for a mark to be strong and thus sustainable.

TM

The ™ symbol designates that the mark owner claims common law trademark rights, and that the mark has not been formerly registered.

For insuring a strong mark, there are two basic approaches. The first is to make the mark very distinctive. The more distinctive the trademark, the stronger the protection afforded its use. Fanciful marks, which utilize made-up words such as Exxon and Xerox, are good examples of such distinctive marks. Another type of distinctive trademark is a mark that is classified as arbitrary. Arbitrary marks are those in which common words are applied in ways that are out of place, such as the word Apple with Macintosh computers. Fanciful and arbitrary trademarks are considered very strong marks.

TRADEMARKS

SM

The ᴸᴹ symbol designates that the mark relates to a service rather than a product.

The second approach to having a strong mark is to use and advertise the mark in commerce. An example of this type of acquired distinctiveness is found with Microsoft's Windows operating system. In the early 1980s, when the word "windows" was adopted by Microsoft as a trademark for their new operating system, the mark was extremely weak, and thought by many to be unprotectable. After nearly 30 years of intense advertising and legal policing, however, the Windows mark has acquired distinctiveness and strength and has since been registered with the USPTO.

Unlike certain other forms of intellectual property, trademarks grow stronger with use, and in fact, trademark rights can lapse if a mark is not properly used and cared

Trademarks can be lost if not properly used and policed.

for. Specifically, if a trademark has not been used for three consecutive years in commerce, it is presumed to be abandoned. For instance, the Trademark Serial Number 78043745 was registered on May 7, 1999, by Microsoft to be used on bathrobes, caps, and nightshirts, etc. However, because Microsoft never actively pursued this mark, it was abandoned three years later.

TRADEMARKS

United States of America
United States Patent and Trademark Office

Google

Reg. No. 4,123,471
Registered Apr. 10, 2012
Int. Cl.: 35

SERVICE MARK
PRINCIPAL REGISTER

GOOGLE INC. (DELAWARE CORPORATION)
2400 BAYSHORE PARKWAY
TRADEMARK DEPT
MOUNTAIN VIEW, CA 94043

FOR: DISSEMINATION OF ADVERTISING FOR OTHERS VIA THE INTERNET, IN CLASS 35 (U.S. CLS. 100, 101 AND 102).

FIRST USE 10-0-2000; IN COMMERCE 10-0-2000.

THE MARK CONSISTS OF STANDARD CHARACTERS WITHOUT CLAIM TO ANY PARTICULAR FONT, STYLE, SIZE, OR COLOR.

OWNER OF U.S. REG. NOS. 2,806,075 AND 2,884,502.

SER. NO. 78-433,507, FILED 6-10-2004.

PATRICIA EVANKO, EXAMINING ATTORNEY

David J. Kappos
Director of the United States Patent and Trademark Office

A trademark certificate.

Another way that trademarks die is through public misuse. Since trademarks provide identification of a product or service, it is important that the association between the mark and the product remains strong. If the public begins to casually refer to all products of a certain class by a protected name, the trademark status of that name will be lost.

For instance, the Otis Elevator Company lost the trademark on the term *escalator* by casually using the term in advertising instead of moving staircase. Other examples of lost trademarks include *Aspirin* (for pain medication) and *elevator* (for automated lifting device). Xerox nearly lost rights to its trademark in the 1960s, as the process of duplicating a document began to be commonly referred to as "making a Xerox" of the page. Aggressive advertising, education, and policing have greatly strengthened the Xerox mark over the past two decades. Kleenex encountered a similar situation, as the trademark was commonly substituted for tissues.

Fanciful and arbitrary marks are the easiest to assert and protect.

SELECTING A STRONG TRADEMARK

When the time comes to select a strong trademark, conflicts often arise between the marketing professionals' goal to describe or clearly suggest the product, and the trademark

TRADEMARKS

attorneys' counsel that recommends trademarks be completely fanciful or arbitrary. From the marketing perspective, fanciful and arbitrary trademarks totally contradict marketing efforts for easily associating the trademark with the product or service. Much more advertising would be required to teach the public that gas could be purchased at an Exxon store than would be required for a store named Quick Fill. However, from the legal perspective, the Exxon brand is a significantly stronger trademark and would be more easily asserted and protected. The more distinctive the trademark, the stronger the trademark protection.

LEGAL BRIEF: RIGHTS OF A REGISTERED TRADEMARK

- Serves as notice regarding ownership of the trademark; prevents second-party claims of "innocent infringers."

- Grants the right to display the registered symbol ®.

TRADEMARKS

A second issue that is important to consider when selecting a trademark is the meaning the mark may have when translated into foreign languages. Although the mark may be perfectly acceptable when pronounced or recited in the English language, a completely separate connotation may result when translated into a foreign language. A famous example of this translation problem occurred some years ago when Chevrolet adopted the name "Nova" for a model of automobile. The problem occurred when translating Nova in the Latin American market, where the word roughly translates to mean, "it doesn't go." An example of a less lighthearted product naming blunder was when the sportswear company Umbro introduced a sneaker called the "Zyklon." The company was inundated with complaints from organizations and individuals as Zyklon was the name of the gas used by the Nazis in concentration camps. The product was quickly withdrawn from the market. Advertising lore is filled with numerous examples of brands, logos, and trade slogans that produce adverse and, even in some cases, hostile market responses, when their meanings are interpreted among various cultures.

Registered trademarks can be searched by visiting www.uspto.gov.

TRADEMARKS

After a short list of names is selected and vetted for possible use as trademarks, a useful next step is to quickly search prior registrations of the marks within the trademark database of the USPTO, accessible at www.uspto.gov. Although this search does not provide absolute clearance when adopting a trademark, it is a quick check to determine whether some other company or entity has previously registered the mark or is in the process of registering the mark for a related product. A professional trademark search organization should be consulted before adopting a final trademark, particularly when the mark is expected to be widely advertised and promoted.

> **Trademarks protect buyers from confusion and deception.**

WHY DO TRADEMARKS MATTER?

Trademarks distinguish sources of commercial goods and services, and ultimately protect buyers from confusion and deception. Buyers depend on marks visible at the time of purchase to know the maker of the goods. This is particularly true with commodity goods where multiple manufacturers may compete with similar products, and the buying decision is usually made based on the cost and quality of the competing merchandise.

TRADEMARKS

Trademarks are exceedingly important to companies because these marks tie goods to their reputations. A trademark not only concerns the goods that may be competing side by side on one particular shelf, but all other goods produced by the owner also. If a variety of products purchased from the same company by a consumer are of consistently high quality, the company will deservedly earn a reputation for delivering excellent merchandise. The mark associated with the company will then become a symbol of quality that will not only extend to the company's reputation, but to their other products as well.

A company that takes pride in the products it makes and sells, especially those products at the high end of a market, will not want to have the value of those products diminished by cheap knockoffs and counterfeit goods. A reputation is fragile, and when sullied by an inferior product, a poor reputation can work to diminish the value of other products carrying that mark.

A prime example may be found on the streets of New York, where imitation Rolex watches are sold for $20 on a frequent basis. If someone were to buy one of these counterfeits and give it as a gift, the recipient of the gift would be quite disappointed in the presumed quality of a Rolex watch when the counterfeit

TRADEMARKS

watch quickly rusts and falls apart. Of course, the watch owner certainly could not be blamed for denouncing the company's shoddy workmanship to his friends in this circumstance. The last thing Rolex, or any company for that matter, would want is a disillusioned consumer, especially when what he had actually purchased was a cheap imitation. To this end, Rolex protects its brand by implementing several anti-counterfeiting features, such as engraving model and serial numbers on various parts of the watch, laser etching on the crystal, and even clear display backs to showcase the quality interior movement. Given the potential harm, it is understandable that companies should be protective of their trademarks and view their marks as extensions of their reputations.

> **LEGAL BRIEF: WHY DO TRADEMARKS MATTER?**
>
> - Distinguish a company's product or service from competitors.
> - Represent a symbol of quality for other goods or services a company may produce; are linked to a company's reputation.
> - Reputation can be undermined by counterfeit products.

■ CHAPTER FIVE ■

COPYRIGHTS

A copyright is the protection given for creative expression. Copyrights are used to protect artistic and creative works such as songs, paintings, movies, statues, architectural drawings, photographs, and computer programs. Only the expression is protected—facts and ideas are not protected by copyright.

The three basic requirements for a work to be copyrightable are that the work must be: original, fixed in a tangible medium of expression, and at least minimally creative. Although lawyers argue endlessly at the boundaries of the copyright laws, whether something can be copyrighted or is protectable is fairly intuitive. For example, if you compose a song (original work) and either write it down or record the song in a fixed medium (tape, CD, piano roll, non-volatile computer memory, etc.), and the song is at least minimally creative, the song is copyrightable.

Copyrights protect expression, not ideas, facts, or inventions.

As the name suggests, copyright protection precludes others from copying or reproducing the work without permission from the owner, but a copyright owner actually has five exclusive rights with respect to the creative work. These rights include: reproduction (the right to copy), distribution, adaptation (preparing derivative works), performing the work publicly, and displaying the work publicly. Provided that the copyright was registered after January 1, 1978, these exclusive rights exist for the author for the duration of his or her life, plus seventy years. Engaging in any of these activities without a license from the copyright owner during that time period constitutes copyright infringement.

Copyrights last for the life of the author plus seventy years.

Oddly enough, however, one author may legally create a work that is identical to another that is already copyrighted. For instance, a songwriter can legally write a song that is exactly the same as a song that has already been written. The new song can be word for word and note for note identical—as long as the writer did not copy the old song in creating the new work. Even though the likelihood of randomly writing a song identical to another may be statistically remote, two independently created identical works are each entitled to copyright protection. However, if two songs sound similar and the later writer is aware of the previous song, the writer may be found to have subconsciously copied. Singer George Harrison learned this

> **Infringement of a copyrighted work requires actual copying.**

lesson the hard way with his hit single "My Sweet Lord" being too similar to Ronnie Mack's "He's So Fine."

Although seemingly easy to understand, the issues of copyright continue to be abused and misunderstood by the general public. In recent years, for example, an entire subculture has grown up around the practice of peer-to-peer sharing of music and video files. One of the earliest enablers of this activity was a company called Napster. Napster distributed file-sharing software and maintained a website directory of users willing to share music files on their computers by letting other users connect to their computers and download the files. This sharing of music and video files is completely legal so long as those doing the sharing actually own the files that they are allowing to be shared. (This would fall under a copyright owner's right to copy and distribute.)

The issue with the vast majority of Napster users was that they often were sharing no music of their own, but instead exchanging copyrighted songs copied from original CDs, specifically by converting a song from a copyrighted CD to a digital audio file called an MP3. The copyright owners of the songs on the CDs had exclusive rights of copying and distribution and in most cases had not extended those rights to the many users of Napster. Thus, those Napster users were committing copyright *infringement*. After several years of copyright-related court battles, Napster closed its doors to peer-to-peer file sharing in 2002.

Similarly, the distribution of copyrighted video and software files has become a growing problem. In response, the scope of conduct that constitutes criminal copyright law has expanded to include willful infringement (for-profit and not-for-profit) and pre-release piracy

The ℗ symbol designates the ownership of reproduction rights in phono records, tapes, and compact disks.

(e.g., sharing a movie before opening day). The penalties are fairly steep, ranging from one year in prison and a $100,000 fine to three years in prison and a $250,000 fine for a first offense. For example, James Clayton Baxter, owner and operator of various software marketing websites, sold illegal copies of Microsoft and Adobe software at one-fifth the retail price for several years. He was convicted and sentenced to four years in prison and fined more than $400,000.

WHY DO COPYRIGHTS MATTER?

Napster developed an extremely clever model for enabling the wide distribution of information. The exchange of files between

COPYRIGHTS

Certificate of Registration

This Certificate issued under the seal of the Copyright Office in accordance with title 17, *United States Code*, attests that registration has been made for the work identified below. The information on this certificate has been made a part of the Copyright Office records.

Maria A. Pallante

Register of Copyrights, United States of America

Registration Number
VAu 1-090-219

Effective date of registration:
January 30, 2012

Title
- **Title of Work:** James Pratt Dec 2011 to Jan 27 2012

Completion/Publication
- **Year of Completion:** 2012

Author
- **Author:** James Adam Pratt
- **Author Created:** photograph(s)
- **Work made for hire:** No
- **Citizen of:** United States
- **Domiciled in:** United States
- **Year Born:** 1960

Copyright claimant
- **Copyright Claimant:** James Adam Pratt
  1608 Mesa Trail, Edmond, OK, 73025, United States

Rights and Permissions
- **Name:** James Pratt
- **Email:** james@james-pratt.com
- **Telephone:** 405-641-3830
- **Address:** 1608 Mesa Trail
  Edmond, OK 73025 United States

Certification
- **Name:** James Pratt
- **Date:** January 30, 2012

Page 1 of 1

independent, peer-to-peer computer users was revolutionary in terms of creating a huge virtual distribution system for data. Since Napster was not actually copying, storing, or distributing copyrighted music on its website, and since legitimate file sharing was facilitated by the Napster service, a great debate regarding the legality of the Napster model remains.

Copyright violations led to Napster's demise in 2002.

Although Napster was found by the courts to be violating the copyright laws by facilitating this sharing of mostly copyrighted files, the ultimate undoing of Napster was its inability to generate meaningful revenue from its services. Because Napster was not charging for its service of maintaining its directory of users, the company had no long-term way of supporting its operations and paying its employees (and lawyers). The consumer benefit contributed by Napster's software and website was being given away for free; businesses cannot survive on this non-revenue model.

This is one of the reasons why a copyright is so important to a creator of a work. The exclusive rights established by a copyright present a creator with the capability of capitalizing on his or her creation in a multitude of avenues, without concern of unauthorized exploitation—or at least it gives the

COPYRIGHTS

The threshold of originality to claim a copyright is relatively low. creator legal recourse if someone does attempt to exploit his or her work, such as in the Napster case. This ability and protection not only gives the creator the means to continue creating—based on the profitability of his or her creations—but the control over his or her works also serves as an incentive to continue creating. Since copyrights protect an owner against copyright infringement, he

LEGAL BRIEF: EXCLUSIVE RIGHTS OF A COPYRIGHT OWNER

- To make reproductions.

- To prepare derivative works based on pre-existing works, such as a translation, sound recording, motion picture version, or fictionalization.

- To distribute copies by sale or transfer of ownership.

- To perform the work publicly.

- To display the work publicly.

or she can control the application and distribution of the work and ultimately earn a living from his or her efforts.

For instance, a very strong copyright-like interest is held by the U.S. regarding its currency. If the counterfeiting of currency was permitted to go unchecked, money would eventually lose its value, and the general economy would quickly collapse. Similarly, a copyright-like interest was granted by Congress to boat hull manufacturers to protect the ornamental and utilitarian function of a vessel's body. To the copyright owner, the value of the copyrighted work is the same. Without being able to control reproduction, distribution, and the other related rights, the economy of and incentives for owners of creative works would soon collapse.

The Ⓜ symbol designates a mask works registration.

MASK WORKS

A mask work is another right that has a copyright-like interest. It is a two- or three-dimensional arrangement on a semiconductor chip. The term *mask* is used to refer to the process in creating the arrangements on the semiconductor chip. Mask works became protectable rights through the Semiconductor Chip Protection Act of 1984. The protections are limited compared to patents and copyrights; the duration of the mask work right is ten years, and there are no protections for independently created identical masks, or masks derived from the protected work.

OWNERSHIP OF COPYRIGHTS

When a copyrighted work is initially created, the author (or authors) of the work generally is the owner of the copyright.

There are two major exceptions to this author-ownership rule.

The first exception occurs when an employee acting within the scope of employment prepares the work. In this instance, the employer—rather than the employee—owns the work. This is referred to as a *work made for hire*. For example, if Janice is hired as an assistant in the human resources department, one of her responsibilities might include taking snapshots of all new employees for use with their employee badges. Although these photographs are arguably creative works and Janice is the creator of these works, her company owns the copyrights on the pictures once the photos are created within the scope of Janice's employment.

The second exception to author-ownership arises when the work falls into one of nine categories specified by the Copyright

> Company-owned copyrights are protected for ninety-five years from the first date of publication.

COPYRIGHTS

Statute and when there is a written agreement in place that the commissioning party will own the work product. These nine categories include such works as motion pictures, audio-visual works, translations, instructional texts, and the like. One area of exclusion concerns software products, especially when computer programs are written by contractors. Companies often subcontract the writing of software code to third parties. When this subcontracting occurs, it is extremely important to ensure that the copyrightable computer code is properly assigned by the third-party contractor to the commissioning company. This problem is not uncommon in the preparation of websites and programs related to Internet commerce that are written by third parties. Absent writings to the contrary, a subcontracting web designer could legally own the company's Internet website or e-commerce software. This ownership can be particularly troublesome when a decision is made to change web design contractors, or when pricing is negotiated for follow-on work. To avoid questions of ownership, software companies should require a written agreement from all contractors, assigning all work product resulting under the

> Absent a specific writing to the contrary, third-party software developers own the copyrights in the programs they create as contractors.

contract to the company. *See appendix for a sample copyright assignment.*

PROTECTING YOUR COPYRIGHTS

Although no longer a requirement to protect an owner's copyrights, registration of copyrighted works with the United States Copyright Office can provide valuable benefits to the owner. Copyright registration is a relatively straightforward process, requiring the completion of a one- or two-page form and the submission of the application with two complete copies of the best edition of the registered work.

The © symbol designates copyright ownership.

The deposit of two copies of the best edition is in part intended to endow the Library of Congress with copies of all creative works ever registered in the U.S.—the ultimate book, record, and movie collection. The registration fee for electronic filing of basic copyright protection is $35. Registration is important because it provides for the availability of statutory damages, which is monetary compensation for an act of infringement, without having to prove that a monetary loss occurred due to the infringement. The damages are between $750 and $30,000 per work, at the discretion of the court. Registration also provides the added benefit of recovery of potential attorney fees for the infringed registrant.

Since 1989, copyright owners are no longer required to place a written notice on their copyrighted works. The use of the copyright notice, however, still provides useful benefits in the event of copyright litigation since it removes the defense of innocent infringement. A simple copyright notice consists of the © symbol, followed by the year of the publication and the name of the author. For example, ©2014 John S. Ferrell.

CHAPTER SIX

TRADE SECRETS

A trade secret is often defined as nearly any form of information used in one's business that provides an advantage over another who does not know or use it. As an intellectual property right, trade secret protection is a bit of an oddball. Unlike other forms of intellectual property, trade secrets are not registered with the federal government. There is no trade secret application to file and no federal office of trade secret protection.

> Since issued patents are published and available to the public, patents and trade secret protections are mutually exclusive.

Trade secret protection is often the subject of a contract between two parties, such as a Non-Disclosure Agreement (NDA); contract disputes and theft of trade secret accusations are generally heard in state courts and are governed by the laws of the various states.

To qualify for trade secret protection, the "secret" must be of commercial value, not well known, and not easily discernable using legal means. It is also a requirement in most states that reasonable steps be taken to protect the secret.

TRADE SECRETS

To help us explore the contours of trade secrets, imagine you hypothetically invented a remote control levitating device called the "Levitator." You might forego patent protection and choose to keep this handheld levitator mechanism a secret by using it only to move piles of business plans and technical books about your office. However, since its existence and name will only be a secret within your company, there is no need for a trademark on the name. (Indeed, because it is a descriptive mark, the name *Levitator* is not registrable as a trademark.) To make sure you qualify for trade secret protection, you should take every reasonable step to keep the tool a secret, by making sure all parties potentially exposed to the Levitator are aware that its existence is a secret and by making reasonable efforts to keep the knowledge of its existence exclusively among privileged parties. Such reasonable efforts might include locking file cabinets, marking documents confidential, and limiting access to rooms where the trade secret device is used.

Because the Levitator has commercial value and your company is taking reasonable steps to keep the tool a secret, you will be afforded certain protections for this device. These

Public policy encourages legitimate reverse engineering of products to promote the progress of innovation.

TRADE SECRETS

US006960975B1

(12) **United States Patent**
Volfson

(10) Patent No.: **US 6,960,975 B1**
(45) Date of Patent: **Nov. 1, 2005**

(54) **SPACE VEHICLE PROPELLED BY THE PRESSURE OF INFLATIONARY VACUUM STATE**

(76) Inventor: **Boris Volfson**, 5707 W. Maple Grove Rd., Apt. 3046, Huntington, IN (US) 46750

(*) Notice: Subject to any disclaimer, the term of this patent is extended or adjusted under 35 U.S.C. 154(b) by 8 days.

(21) Appl. No.: **11/079,670**

(22) Filed: **Mar. 14, 2005**

Related U.S. Application Data

(63) Continuation of application No. 10/633,778, filed on Aug. 4, 2003, now abandoned.

(51) Int. Cl.[7] **H01F 6/00**; F03H 5/00
(52) U.S. Cl. **335/216**; 60/200.1
(58) Field of Search 335/216; 60/200.1

(56) **References Cited**

U.S. PATENT DOCUMENTS

3,626,615 A	12/1971	Wallace
3,626,606 A	12/1971	Wallace
3,823,570 A	7/1974	Wallace
5,197,279 A	3/1993	Taylor
6,353,311 B1	3/2002	Brainard et al.

OTHER PUBLICATIONS

M.T. French, "To the Stars by Electromagnetic Propulsion", http://www.mtjf.demon.co.uk/antigravp2.htm#cforce.
Evgeny Podkletnov, "Weak Gravitational Shielding Properties of Composite Bulk $YBa_2Cu_3O_{(7-x)}$ Superconductor Below 70K Under E.M. Field", LANL database number cond-mat/9701074, v. 3, 10 pages, Sep. 16, 1997.
N. LI & D.G. Torr, "Effects of a Gravitomagnetic Field on Pure Superconductors", Physical Review, vol. 43, p. 457, 3 pages, Jan. 15, 1991.

Evgeny Podkletnov, Giovanni Modanese "Impulse Gravity Generator Based on Charged $YBa_2Cu_3O_{7-y}$ Superconductor with Composite Crystal Structure", arXiv.org/physics database, #0108005 vol. 2, 32 pages, 8 figures, Aug. 30, 2001.
S. Kopeikin & E. Fomalont, "General Relativistic Model for Experimental Measurement of the Speed of Propagation of Gravity by VLBI", Proceedings of the 6th European VLBI Network Symposium Jun. 25-28, 2002, Bonn, Germany, 4 pages.
Sean M. Carroll, "The Cosmological Constant", http://pancake.uchicago.edu/~carroll/encyc/, 6 pages.
Chris Y. Taylor and Giovanni Modanese, "Evaluation of an Impulse Gravity Generator Based Beamed Propulsion Concept", American Institute of Aeronautics and Astronautics, Inc., 2002.
Peter L. Skeggs, "Engineering Analysis of the Podkletnov Gravity Shielding Experiment", Quantum Forum, Nov. 7, 1997, http://www.inetarena'.com/~noetic/pls/podlev.html).

Primary Examiner—Ramon M. Barrera

(57) **ABSTRACT**

A space vehicle propelled by the pressure of inflationary vacuum state is provided comprising a hollow superconductive shield, an inner shield, a power source, a support structure, upper and lower means for generating an electromagnetic field, and a flux modulation controller.

A cooled hollow superconductive shield is energized by an electromagnetic field resulting in the quantized vortices of lattice ions projecting a gravitomagnetic field that forms a spacetime curvature anomaly outside the space vehicle. The spacetime curvature imbalance, the spacetime curvature being the same as gravity, provides for the space vehicle's propulsion. The space vehicle, surrounded by the spacetime anomaly, may move at a speed approaching the light-speed characteristic for the modified locale.

13 Claims, 6 Drawing Sheets

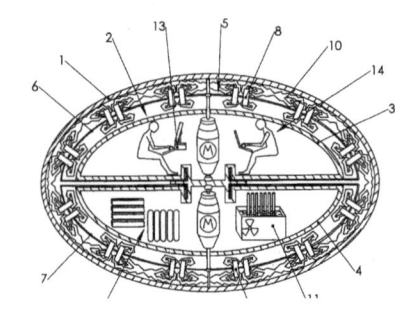

TRADE SECRETS

protections include: rights against disclosure of the trade secret by those who may obtain it by improper means, such as a thief breaking into your company; disclosure of the trade secret by those privileged parties who are aware that the information is a valuable secret, such as confidential employees; or, another party learning of the secret (with the knowledge that it is a secret) when disclosure to him or her was made by mistake.

> A non-disclosure agreement is a secrecy contract between at least two parties.

On the other hand, if you choose to leverage your advantage with this remote by selling the Levitator tool at the neighborhood Kmart, your trade secret claims will be surrendered since you will be ceasing efforts to keep it a secret. Once a Kmart shopper purchases the gadget, she is free to take it apart and figure out how it works. This process of reverse engineering is not only legal, but encouraged, since our society has a strong interest in furthering technological improvement. Unless you have other intellectual property protections covering the Levitator device, the industrious Kmart shopper can study and tweak your design and sell an improved levitation remote to all of your competitors, thus completely neutralizing your earlier business advantage.

TRADE SECRETS

The more typical use of trade secret protection comes into play when two businesses collaborate to explore a joint opportunity. Elaborating on the Levitator example, say a competing company might reside on an adjacent floor of your firm's building. Their business manager might approach you and offer to enter into an agreement to share library resources. As part of this agreement, both parties would execute a contract outlining the details of how this library sharing arrangement will work. Part of this agreement might include an NDA in which you both agree not to disclose any trade secrets that are learned from the other. Specifically cited in an exhibit to this section of the agreement is a description of your secret Levitator equipment, used for lifting and moving books and business papers.

The book sharing arrangement works wonderfully for a year or so, until one day, while shopping for office supplies at the local Kmart, much to your horror and dismay, you run across a display of Levitator remotes. Not only has your levitation apparatus been heisted by some trade-secret-stealing ne'er-do-well, but your beloved pet name has also been lifted.

By simply inspecting the product packaging, you find that the manufacturer of these knock-off levitators is none other than…the company upstairs, your book club buddies, and cosignators of the NDA the prior year. This would be a clear breach of your agreement not to disclose each other's trade secrets and grounds for a claim against your neighbor for breach of contract and theft of your trade secret.

WHY DO TRADE SECRETS MATTER?

Trade secrets are important to recognize because they reward competitive ingenuity in the marketplace. For instance,

> **LEGAL BRIEF: RIGHTS OF A TRADE SECRET**
>
> - Protect against third parties obtaining the secret via improper acquisition.
>
> - Protect against privileged parties, such as employees, knowingly disclosing the secret.
>
> - Protect against a third party knowingly learning of the secret when the disclosure was made to him or her by mistake.

if the Levitator had been kept a secret, your competitiveness against other similar businesses would have had the added edge of heightened efficiency and lower costs in running your business.

Trade secrets also enable businesses to engage more freely in a broader range of activities with their employees, vendors, customers, and other businesses. If an employee of your firm could leave and legally take all the secrets that he learned during his employment, especially your prized Levitator, you would soon have no secrets left. With trade secret protections, your employees can work together as a team with reduced concern about losing your business advantages through others within the company.

Trade secret protection improves business efficiency.

Trade secret protection reduces unnecessary wastefulness of effort that results if such protections are not in place. As in the Levitator example, certain opportunities are not possible if businesses cannot protect secrets that are necessarily disclosed in such arrangements. In the Levitator example, if you proceed with the book-sharing arrangement without such protections, you will have to use the Levitator discreetly, and probably less efficiently, to avoid revealing its existence to the other firm.

Fortunately, however, trade secret protections afford a variety of civil (non-criminal) remedies if a privileged party improperly exploits the knowledge of a trade secret. In addition to the civil remedies available, the Economic Espionage Act of 1996 makes the theft of trade secrets a federal crime. One of the earliest cases of this act involved Patrick Worthing, a maintenance worker at PPG Industries, Inc. He collected disks, blueprints, and other confidential information during his employment and, with his brother Daniel, attempted to sell the information to Owens-Corning, PPG's competitor. He pleaded guilty in 1997 and was sentenced to fifteen months in prison. His brother received sixty months probation and six months home confinement.

"MORNING-AFTER PILL" FOR NDAs

When sharing your trade secret with others, there are times when the receiving party may refuse to sign an NDA. For example, venture capitalists (VCs) will seldom execute NDAs when considering the funding of new start-ups. Most VCs receive hundreds of new venture proposals each year, and managing so many secrets is often impractical for a small funding group.

More importantly, few true start-ups have the negotiating

clout to dictate disclosure terms. If you are trying to get a thirty-minute showing with a potential investor, it's just not good business to spend the first twenty-nine minutes negotiating an NDA.

When negotiating with big companies, the problem may be just plain bureaucracy. Often business units within a company are required by policy to send all contracts to their internal legal departments to review and approve. Many, though not all, company legal departments are understaffed risk management organizations. Tasked with handling everything from defending employee lawsuits to clearing corporate communications, NDAs often move glacially through the approval process. Those on the business front lines of big companies will either insist on using their own one-sided, pre-approved forms, or simply refuse to consider NDAs.

One suggestion for negotiating with big companies is a technique called the *post-facto NDA*. The post-facto NDA is like the morning-after pill for invention disclosure. If you are refused a signature on your NDA form, or for whatever reason you decide that asking for an NDA signature is not appropriate at the time, explain to the receiving party that you want to share your invention with them and ask politely if the invention could be shared with them in confidence. Almost always, someone

TRADE SECRETS

who is asked whether you can share your secret with them in confidence will answer affirmatively. There is something about human nature that if someone is asked whether they can keep a secret, it is almost impossible for them to say no. If, in fact, you ask the question, "Can I share my invention

> **LEGAL BRIEF: WHY DO TRADE SECRETS MATTER**
>
> - Reward competitive ingenuity in the marketplace.
>
> - Enable businesses to engage in activities much more freely, such as with employees, vendors, customers, and other businesses.
>
> - Reduce unnecessary wastefulness of effort that otherwise would be needed to protect such secrets.

TRADE SECRETS

Non-disclosure agreements are used to contractually agree to retain confidentiality of exchanged trade secrets.

with you in confidence?" and the answer is no, you should seriously consider whether the receiving party has an interest in hearing about your invention.

Once you get the verbal agreement to share the invention in confidence, go ahead and disclose the invention to them at a level that you feel necessary. The way the post-facto NDA works is that the next day, or as soon as is convenient, send the receiving party a letter, thanking them for taking the time to listen to your invention disclosure and for agreeing to keep your invention in confidence. This letter creates a record of the verbal agreement to exchange your secret for their promise to keep it. In effect, you have a written record of the oral NDA previously made. Keep a copy, as this letter of an oral contract can provide powerful evidence in the event that a dispute over the invention disclosure ever arises.

PROTECTING TRADE SECRETS

Really good trade secrets are very hard to keep. Like trying to store JELL-O in a birdcage, there are one hundred ways that secrets can slip out, and without vigilance and education, the cage will be forever empty. An effective trade secret

November 15, 2008

Mr. William Doe
Street Address
City, State ZIP

Re: Post-meeting Follow-up on POOL PARADISE

Dear Bill:

Thank you very much for meeting with me yesterday to discuss my new outdoor lounger concept that I have tentatively labeled POOL PARADISE. As I mentioned at our meeting, I have not yet gone public with this technology and appreciate your agreeing to keep this confidential until I do so.

This outdoor lounger would be a terrific addition to your lineup of products, and should be an easy match for your existing manufacturing processes. I would be happy to explore with you further your idea of manufacturing the lounger in other materials. Perhaps you could send me some sample plastic swatches from your supplier.

I'm looking forward to getting together again with you and your team at the upcoming WaterWorld conference in Reno next month. Until then, please don't hesitate to call if you would like to accelerate discussions.

Sincerely,

John S. Ferrell

program requires more than just NDAs. For the secret to be well protected, several elements should be in place, including a written policy, documentation of the secret, appointment of a curator, education, and policing.

Effective trade secret programs begin with a written policy that clearly sets forth the processes within the organization indicating how trade secrets will be recognized and preserved. The written trade secret policy also serves as a basis for education and trade secret policing. The policy should be clear and easily understood, and it should apply to all employees and all vendors.

Recording trade secrets is a key step to their protection.

In order to protect secrets, it is important to identify them. Especially in larger companies, it is essential to record the trade secrets and keep a record of where and how the secrets are used. Although this may seem a bit counterintuitive, it is impossible to protect a secret that no one knows. Recording the secret serves the dual purpose of identifying the importance of the information, while at the same time preventing the loss of the secret through neglect and the passage of time.

To execute the written policy and to store and preserve the secrets, a specific person in the company should be assigned to be the curator and the guardian of the trade secret jewels. Often

TRADE SECRETS

the curator of trade secrets is someone in the company's legal department. In smaller companies, this responsibility might fall on the chief technology officer or an engineering fellow of the company. It is helpful to appoint someone who will have a general understanding of the secret and will be able to recognize where and when the secret is being used or misused.

> **Include vendors in trade secret training.**

Education requires that all employees be regularly briefed and reminded of the trade secret policy. This is especially important when considering the role that vendors play within the company. Vendors are the worker bees of industry. They facilitate productivity and growth and enable businesses to bloom and prosper. But like bees that move from plant to plant, vendors can also inadvertently move important trade secrets among the companies they service. To guard against this, employees interacting with the vendors must ultimately be charged with the responsibility of training vendors on trade secret management. When new products are being developed, it is important to emphasize to all vendors, preferably in writing, which elements of the development are confidential and frequently remind them of the importance of protecting the company's confidences.

Ongoing policing of trade secrets is the most important

aspect of the preservation mechanism. Surprisingly, many of the policing objectives can be accomplished with simple efforts. Avoid keeping visitor logs at the reception desk—use sign-in cards instead. It's often a simple matter to deduce the activities of a company by viewing a visitor log to see who has visited whom, and the purpose(s) of the visit(s). Other simple methods for policing trade secrets might include: restricting the dissemination of important trade secrets to small groups of need-to-know people; limiting the transmission of trade secrets via email, thus reducing the risk of accidental broadcasting; and, using NDAs with all outside parties when revealing trade secrets. Although the NDAs will not ultimately prevent intentional theft, the ceremony of signing such an agreement acts as a cautionary reminder to those well-intentioned business partners.

> **Use sign-in cards rather than visitor logs in company reception areas to prevent the disclosure of prior visitors.**

CHAPTER SEVEN

CONCLUSION

Willis Carrier was a phenomenally creative inventor—his indoor air-conditioning technology is credited with saving the lives of countless people and improving the lives of many more. Intellectual property protection doubtlessly played little or no role in his genius but likely was pivotal in the success of the Carrier company. It was the protection afforded to Willis' inventions, and the competitive advantages and temporary monopolies that this Intellectual Property protection provided, that enabled the Carrier company to launch and grow and improve their commercial products.

Patents provided Willis with protection for technology inventions and improvements. He filed his first patent application in 1906, and it was with these early patents that he was able to raise the money to launch the new Carrier venture a decade later. Patents created exclusionary monopolies for this fledging company to prevent others from making, using or selling the patented invention, providing Willis an opportunity to exploit and commercialize the products of his intellectual efforts. Over the years, patents have protected not only the

CONCLUSION

mechanical structures of Carrier's air-conditioning machines, but also methods for using and building the equipment, as well as processes and methods for filtering and treating air in general.

In the same way that patents helped Carrier launch the air-conditioning industry in the early twentieth century, the protections they provide are exceedingly important to new ventures of the present. The product monopolies that are created with strategically engineered patents create breathing room for the company to sell its products, unrivaled by price-slashing competitors trying to gain market share at the expense of profits. In addition to providing barriers to competition for start-up companies with new innovations, patents also encourage outside investment. Patents validate the novelty of a technology for investors and also provide concrete assets that will remain when assigned to the company, even if founders or other inventors leave the start-up for bluer skies.

But not all great innovations necessarily require patents. In 1886, Dr. John Pemberton of Atlanta—perhaps the most celebrated pharmacist of all time—mixed a secret recipe of coca leaves and kola nuts to create the headache-reducing elixir Coca-Cola®. This fragrant mixture was initially served by the glass, mixed with chilled soda water, to customers of Jacob's Pharmacy in Atlanta, Georgia. Although the mixture was

CONCLUSION

certainly suitable for patenting, Pemberton and later owners of the secret formula chose to protect the formulation (called *7X*) as a trade secret, disclosing the recipe only to a small group of trusted employees and associates.

The most valuable asset that Pemberton and his successors developed over the years, however, was the Coca-Cola brand. The Coca-Cola name was first registered with the U.S. Trademark Office in 1893, and over the years has become one of the strongest trademarks in the world. With slogans such as "Things go better with Coke," "It's the Real Thing," and "I'd like to buy the world a Coke," trademark protection has contributed to building a brand worth billions of dollars.

John Pemberton, inventor of Coca-Cola.

BUNDLE OF RIGHTS

Intellectual property can be protected in a variety of ways; owners of creations are often said to possess a bundle of rights. The exact composition of the bundle depends upon the nature and scope of the creation. Pemberton easily could have patented the formula for Coca-Cola, but instead chose to retain the formula as a trade secret. Design patents have been used to protect the various bottle shapes and other Coke containers. Trademark rights play a prominent role in the Coke bundle, as does copyright protection.

When analyzing your creative work think in terms of who might be interested in using your creation and how that use might be made. Is the function of the creation new and patentable, or is this a creative expression that would more appropriately be protected by copyright? Is it possible to seek both? (A software program, for example, might be protectable by both patent and copyright.) Is branding an important part of selling your product? If so, trademark protection is an important consideration. Some products contain ingredients, or are constructed using processes, that are best protected as a trade secret. Keep in mind that patents and trade secrets are mutually exclusive forms of protection, since patents require a full disclosure of the protected technology.

THE BUSINESS DECISION

Ultimately, however, what and how to protect intellectual property should be considered in the context of the business owning the creation. Intellectual property protection has inherent costs. Patents are especially expensive. As in every business decision, it is essential to view every expense in terms

CONCLUSION

of the profit the expense will generate. A patent is only valuable if the benefit to the business from owning the patent exceeds the cost of procurement by an acceptable margin of profit. If the patent does not drive additional sales or protect the product market in some financially tangible way, it's not a worthwhile investment. Likewise, if the creation is commercially valuable, intellectual property protection can create extraordinary returns.

APPENDIX

■ ■ ■

SAMPLE NON-DISCLOSURE AGREEMENT

This Non-Disclosure Agreement (the "**Agreement**") is effective as of ____ day of _____, 20__ (the "**Effective Date**") by and between xxx ("**xxx**" or "**Disclosing Party**"), a Delaware corporation, with its principal place of business at _____, USA and the person or entity named on the signature page hereto ("**Receiving Party**") with his / its principal place of business set forth on the signature page hereto, for the purpose of preventing the unauthorized use and disclosure of Confidential Information (as defined below) which may be disclosed by xxx. xxx and Receiving Party are referred to collectively herein as the "**Parties**" or individually as a "**Party**".

1. Definition of Confidential Information. "Confidential Information" shall mean any and all technical and non-technical information disclosed in writing, orally or by demonstration or delivery of tangible items, including but not limited to trade secret and proprietary information, techniques, sketches, drawings, models, inventions, know-how, processes, apparatus, equipment, software programs, software source documents, product, service and training plans, designs, procurement requirements, purchasing information, customer lists, product and service costs, prices and names, financial information, business and marketing plans, business opportunities, research, technology, experimental work,

APPENDIX

development design details and specifications, and personnel information, including confidential information disclosed by third parties. Without limiting the generality of the foregoing, Confidential Information shall include, but not be limited to, all information specified in **Exhibit A** attached hereto. Confidential Information shall not include information that (A) is now or subsequently becomes generally available to the public through no fault or breach on the part of the Receiving Party; (B) the Receiving Party had rightfully in its possession prior to disclosure by the Disclosing Party to the Receiving Party; (C) is independently developed by the Receiving Party by persons without access to any Confidential Information; or (D) the Receiving Party rightfully obtains without confidentiality restrictions from a third party who has the right to transfer or disclose it. If the Receiving Party claims that Confidential Information received by it is subject to any of the exclusions contained in clauses (A) through (D) above, it shall have the burden of establishing the applicability of such exclusion by documentary evidence.

2. **Non-Disclosure and Non-Use of Confidential Information.** The Receiving Party shall hold and maintain the Confidential Information in strict confidence and for the sole and exclusive benefit of the Disclosing Party as it relates to the actual or contemplated business relationship between the Parties. The Receiving Party shall not, without the prior written approval of the Disclosing Party in each instance or unless otherwise expressly permitted in this Agreement, use for its own benefit, publish or otherwise disclose to others,

APPENDIX

or permit others to use any of the Confidential Information. The Receiving Party shall carefully restrict access to the Confidential Information to those of its employees, consultants and agents who clearly need such access in order to participate on behalf of the Receiving Party in the actual or contemplated business relationship between the Parties and who are bound by written confidentiality agreements that protect the confidentiality and use of such information. The Receiving Party shall not reproduce Confidential Information, in whole or in part, except as necessary for internal use, as provided in this Agreement, nor remove, or cause to be removed, any identification affixed to Confidential Information indicating its proprietary nature. The Receiving Party may disclose Confidential Information if required by any judicial or governmental requirement or order; provided that the Receiving Party will take reasonable steps to give the Disclosing Party sufficient prior notice of such request for the Disclosing Party to contest such requirement or order or to obtain confidential treatment of the Confidential Information by the government, as applicable.

3. No Modification. The Receiving Party agrees that it will not modify, reverse engineer or create other works from any software programs contained in the Confidential Information or decompile or disassemble any such software programs or attempt to do any of the foregoing.

4. Ownership of Confidential Information. All Confidential Information and all intellectual property rights therein remain the property of the Disclosing

APPENDIX

Party, and, except as expressly provided herein, no license or other right to Confidential Information is granted or implied hereby. The Disclosing Party shall have no obligation under this Agreement to supply Confidential Information to the Receiving Party. The Disclosing Party does not warrant or guarantee the accuracy or completeness of any information disclosed pursuant to this Agreement. Accordingly, the Disclosing Party shall have no liability to the Receiving Party or any other entity with respect to the accuracy, completeness or non-realization of any information, including any estimates or projections, disclosed hereunder, nor for the use of, or any reliance on, such information.

5. **Term.** The term of this Agreement shall extend from the Effective Date through the date which is one (1) year from such date, unless earlier terminated by either Party by written notice to the other Party. However, the Receiving Party's duty to protect the Disclosing Party's Confidential Information as set forth herein shall survive for five (5) years from the later of: (i) the Effective Date; or (ii) the date of disclosure of Confidential Information hereunder.

6. **Injunctive Relief.** The Receiving Party understands and acknowledges that any disclosure or misappropriation of any of the Confidential Information in violation of this Agreement may cause the Disclosing Party irreparable harm, the amount of which may be difficult to ascertain and, therefore, agrees that the Disclosing Party shall have the right to apply to a court

APPENDIX

of competent jurisdiction for an order restraining any such further disclosure or misappropriation and for such other relief as the Disclosing Party shall deem appropriate.

7. Return of Confidential Information. Upon termination of this Agreement or at any time upon receipt of a written request from the Disclosing Party, the Receiving Party shall immediately return to the Disclosing Party all written Confidential Information of the Disclosing Party and any and all records, notes and other written, printed, magnetic or tangible materials pertaining to such Confidential Information.

8. No Export. The Receiving Party will not export outside the United States, if a United States company or citizen, or reexport, if a foreign company or citizen, any Confidential Information or direct product thereof, except as permitted by the United States Export Administration Act and regulations thereunder.

9. Binding on Successors. Except as otherwise provided herein, this Agreement and the Receiving Party's obligations hereunder shall be binding upon the representatives, assigns and successors of the Receiving Party and shall inure to the benefit of the assigns and successors of the Disclosing Party. The Receiving Party shall not transfer the Confidential Information, or any rights or obligations hereunder, to any third party without the prior written consent of the Disclosing Party.

10. Governing Law. This Agreement shall be governed by and construed in accordance with the laws of the United States and the internal laws of the State of California.

APPENDIX

11. Remedies. Any and all remedies herein expressly conferred upon a party shall be deemed cumulative with and not exclusive of any other remedy conferred hereby or by law on such party, and the exercise of any one remedy shall not preclude the exercise of any other.

12. Attorneys' Fees. Should suit be brought to enforce or interpret any part of this Agreement, the prevailing party shall be entitled to recover its reasonable attorneys' fees to be fixed by the court (including without limitation fees on any appeal).

13. Entire Agreement. This Agreement constitutes the entire understanding of the Parties with respect to the subject matter hereof and may not be amended or modified except in a writing signed by each of the Parties.

IN WITNESS WHEREOF, the Parties have entered into this Agreement as the Effective Date.

xxx.

By: _____
Printed Name: _____
Title: _____

RECEIVING PARTY:

_____ [a corporation / an individual]

By: _____
Printed Name: _____
Title: _____

Principal Place of Business:
_____
_____
_____
_____

EXHIBIT A

CERTAIN CONFIDENTIAL INFORMATION

APPENDIX

Assignment of Copyright

_____ ("Assignor") hereby assigns to _____ ("Assignee"), the entire right, title, and interest, including all copyrights, and any registrations and renewals thereof, in and to _____ (attached hereto for reference), including all text, artwork, photography, and other authorship therein (collectively, the "Works").

The preceding assignment of copyrights shall include all rights incident to copyright ownership to the maximum extent of applicable law (including judicial or statutory law or other legal authority of the United States or any other country in the world, or under any treaty to which any of the foregoing countries may be a party), for all the residue now unexpired of the present term of any and all such copyrights and any term that may thereafter be granted during which the Works are entitled to copyright, together with all claims for damages by reason of past infringement of said copyrights, with the right to sue and recover for the same for the use and benefit of Assignee. Assignor assigns to Assignee any moral rights he/she/it holds in the Works, and waives and agrees never to assert such rights against Assignee in any jurisdiction.

This assignment is made for good and valuable consideration, receipt of which is hereby acknowledged.

This assignment is effective as of _____, _____.

Signature: _____ Date Signed: _____

INDEX

A

acceptable margin of profit, 95
acquired distinctiveness, 56
AIA, 24. *See also* America Invents Act
air-conditioning, 2, 3, 4, 91, 92
"Apparatus for Treating Air", 4
America Invents Act, 24. *See also* AIA
American patent system, 18, 19, 20, 23
Anthrax, 14
Apple, 55. *See also* Macintosh
articles of manufacture, 52
asexually reproducing plants, 29, 31, 52
assignment of copyright, 102
"Assignee", 102
"Assignor", 102
the "Works", 102
attorney, 22, 49, 50, 51, 59, 75, 101
Attorney General, 22
audio-visual works, 73

author-ownership, 72
exceptions
exclusion categories, 72, 73
work made for hire, 72

B

ball and chain, 45
bargained exchange, 14
bargaining chip, 46
Baxter, James Clayton, 67
biogenetic material, 37
branding (logos), 94
British patent system, 21
Brunelleschi, Filippo, 19, 20
bundle of rights, 93
bureaucracy, 25, 84
business advantage, 9, 12, 48, 79, 82

C

Carrier, 1, 4, 7, 91, 92
Carrier Engineering Corporation, 4
Carrier, Willis Haviland.

INDEX

See Carrier
Chevrolet, 60
 Nova, 60
Ciprofloxacin, 14
civil remedies, 83
Coca-Cola, 9, 92, 93
 Coke, 9, 54, 93, 94
 inventor of, 93. *See also* Pemberton, John
cold fusion, 38
commercial value, 47, 76, 77
common law, 21, 54, 55
computer, 2, 37, 48, 49, 55, 64, 66, 69, 73
confidential employees, 79
confidentiality, 86, 97, 98
Congress, 8, 22, 71, 74
Constitution, 7, 8, 22
contractors, 73
copyright, 8, 9, 12, 64, 65, 66, 67, 69, 70, 71, 72, 73, 74, 75, 94, 102
 assignment, 74
 author-ownership, 72
 copyright-like, 71
 duration, 65
 electronic filing, 74
 exclusion categories, 72–75
 exclusive rights, 65, 69–114
  adaptation, 65
  displaying publicly, 65, 70
  distribution, 65–114
  performing publicly, 65, 70
  reproduction, 65, 67, 70–114, 71
 infringement, 65–67, 70, 74, 102
  Baxter, James Clayton, 67
  Harrison, George, 65
  Napster, 66–67, 69–70
 litigation, 75
 mask works, 71–73
 notice, 75, 98–99
 ownership, 15, 54, 59, 67, 70, 72, 73, 74, 102
 protection, 64–65, 70–72, 74
 registration, 71, 102
 requirements, 64
copyrightable, 64, 73
Copyright Statute, 72–74
 nine categories, 72
cost of preparing and filing, 50–52
counterfeiting, 63, 71
creative expression, 8, 12, 64, 94
curator, 88, 89

D

derivative works, 65, 70
design patents, 9, 29, 30, 52, 94

INDEX

differentiating features, 48
disclosure, 79, 84, 86, 96, 97
documentation of the secret, 88

E

E-commerce, 73
Economic Espionage Act of 1996, 83
exclusive rights, 18–20, 21–22, 31, 65–67, 69
Exxon, 55, 59

F

filed patent claims, 50
first to invent system, 24
flash of genius, 3, 24
Franklin, Benjamin, 8
  Ben Franklin, 8
Fuddruckers, Inc., 54

G

General Welfare Board, 20
Gershwin, George, 53
  Rhapsody in Blue, 53

H

Harrison, George, 65
  "My Sweet Lord", 66
Hippodamus, 19

Hopkins, Samuel, 22
human organisms, 24, 44

I

improper acquisition, 81
infringement, 48, 65–66, 70, 74, 102
instructional texts, 73
intangible creations, 12
intangible property, 7
  trade secrets, 8. *See also* trade secrets
intellectual creation, 7
intellectual property, 7–10, 12, 29–30, 56, 76, 79, 91, 93–95, 98
  copyrights, 8. *See also* copyright
  IP, 7
  patent, 8
  trademarks, 8. *See also* trademark
  trade secrets, 8. *See also* trade secrets
internet, 16, 25, 73
invention, 4, 8–9, 12–13, 15, 19, 22, 24–25, 29–30, 36–38, 45–49, 50–51, 64, 84–86, 91, 96
  ornamental, 9, 12, 13, 30, 52, 71
  protection, 13, 15, 24, 29,

INDEX

47, 48
   selling, 13, 79, 91, 94
   stealth, 47, 48
IP, 7. *See also* intellectual property
issue fee, 51
Ivins, Molly, 1

J

Jack in the Box, 53
Jacob's Pharmacy, 92
Jefferson, Thomas, 23
joint opportunity, 80

K

key technologies, 47
Kleenex, 58
Kmart, 79–81

L

laws of nature, 44
lawsuit, 37, 84
legal briefs, 12, 52, 59, 63, 70, 81, 85
letters patent, 21, 22
levitation apparatus, 80
Levitator, 77, 79–81, 82
Library of Congress, 74
licensee, 37
limited monopolies, 45
look and feel, 30, 54, 55
lost trademarks, 58

M

Mack, Ronnie, 66
   "He's So Fine", 66
maintenance fees, 50–52
mask, 71. *See also* mask works
mask works, 71
   Semiconductor Chip Protection Act, 71
mechanical patent applications, 51
merits of the invention, 37
MGM lion, 54
Microsoft, 56, 67
Microsoft Windows, 56
modeling and prototyping, 30
modern American patent system, 18, 20, 23
monopolies, 8, 13–15, 18–20, 44, 91–93
   exclusionary, 91
   grants, 21
   of foods, 18
   ownership, 15
   rights, 8, 20
   system, 19–20
morning-after pill, 83
motion pictures, 73
MP3, 66

N

Napster, 66–67, 69–70
Nazis, 60

INDEX

NBC peacock, 53
NDAs, 83–84, 88, 90. *See also* non-disclosure agreement
Newman, Joseph, 38
Newton, Sir Isaac, 44
Nobel Prize, 47
non-disclosure agreement, 76, 79, 86, 96. *See also* NDAs
non-obvious designs, 52
non-obvious inventions, 52
non-obviousness requirement, 23
Nova, 60

O

offering to sell, 13
office action, 50
online patent database, 45
online reverse auction, 15–16
origin, 12
ornamental inventions, 9, 12–13
Otis Elevator Company, 58
Owens-Corning, 54, 83

P

patentability, 24, 38
   flash of genius, 3, 24
   synergism, 24
patentable inventions, 47, 49
Patent Act of 1790, 22

patent application, 29–31, 35–38, 44, 47, 49, 50, 91
   provisional, 31, 35–37
patents, 4, 8–9, 15–17, 18–21, 22, 25, 29, 30, 35, 38–39, 45–47, 50, 72, 76, 91–92, 94
   bargaining chip, 46
   five major benefits, 45
      bargaining chip, 45
      control over markets, 46
      limited monopolies, 45
      measure of research, 45
      protection, 45
   patent applications, 29–31, 49–51, 91
   patent claims, 24, 36, 49, 50
   patent monopoly, 13, 14, 21
   patent portfolios, 47
   patent protection, 13–14, 47, 77
   patent term, 15
Pemberton, John, 92, 93
plant patents, 29, 31, 35, 52
point of novelty, 49
policing, 56, 58, 88–90
Polycom SoundStation, 30, 33
post-facto NDA, 84, 86
PPG Industries, Inc., 83
pre-existing works, 70
pre-release piracy, 67
preservation mechanism, 90
Priceline.com, 15–16

INDEX

products, 4, 7, 15–16, 45–48, 52–53, 58, 61–63, 73, 77, 87, 89, 91–92, 94
   Development output, 46
   Features, 46
   Plans, 46–47
   Roadmaps, 47
   Shapes, 54
Progress of Science and useful Arts, 7–8, 22
public consumption, 44
public misuse, 58

Q

Queen's Bench, 21
quid pro quo, 22
quiet period, 45

R

recorded creative expression, 12
registered patent agent, 49
registered symbol, 59
registration, 23, 54, 61, 71, 74, 102
registration fee, 74
reproduction, 31, 65, 67, 70–71
   The right to copy, 65
reproduction rights, 67
reverse engineering, 77, 79
risk management, 84

Rolex, 62–63

S

Sackett-Wilhelms Lithographing Company, 3
sample non-disclosure agreement, 96
San Antonio, Texas, 55
second-party claims, 54, 59
Semiconductor Chip Protection Act of 1984, 71
slogans, 60, 93
smells, 54
software, 7, 66–67, 69, 73, 94, 96, 98
speakerphone, 30, 33
Statute of Monopolies, 21
statutory benefits, 54
statutory damages, 74
stealth inventions, 47–48
strategic patenting, 46
Supreme Court, 24
symbol, 62–63, 74
   copyright, 75
   mask works, 71
   reproduction rights, 67
   service, 56
   trademark, 53
symbols, 53–55, 59, 67, 71, 74–75
synergism, 24

INDEX

T

Taco Cabana, 55
tangible measure of
  research, 46
tax liability, 44
temporary exclusivity, 13
temporary monopolies, 13
threshold of originality, 70
trade marks
  curator, 88–89
trademarks, 8, 9, 10, 12, 24,
    25, 53, 54, 55, 56, 58, 59,
    60, 61, 63, 93, 94
  certificate, 57
  confusion, 53, 61
  database, 61
  famous trademarks, 10
  protection, 94
  registered, 60
trade names, 53
trade secret protection, 76, 77,
    80
trade secrets, 8–9, 76–77, 79,
    80–83, 86, 88–89, 93–94,
    96
  appointment of a
      curator, 88
  competitive ingenuity, 81,
      85
  curator, 88–90
  documentation of the
      secret, 88
  guardian, 88
  management, 89
  policing, 88–90
  protection, 76–90
  training, 89
  written policy, 88
Two Pesos, 55

U

Umbro, 60
unauthorized exploitation, 69
United Airlines, 54
United States Copyright
    Office, 74
U.S. Constitution, 7–8, 22
U.S. Department of
    Commerce, 24
U.S. government-permitted
    monopoly, 14
USPTO, 9, 24–25, 27, 35, 38,
    44, 45, 49, 50, 51, 54, 56,
    61
U.S. Trademark Office, 93
utility patents, 13, 29, 30, 31,
    50, 52

V

valuation, 15, 16
VCs, 83. *See also* venture
    capitalists
vendors, 82, 85, 88, 89
venture capitalists, 83

INDEX

W

Weathermaker. *See* Carrier
Wendy's, 53
windfall, 14, 15
work made for hire
    See copyright
Worthing, Patrick, 83
written notice, 75, 99

X

Xerox, 55, 58

Z

Zeno, 19
Zyklon, 60

About the Author

■ ■ ■

John S. Ferrell is a founding partner of Menlo Park-based Carr & Ferrell LLP, one of Silicon Valley's foremost intellectual property and corporate law firms.

Listed by the *Los Angeles Daily Journal* as one of **California's Top Rainmakers**, Ferrell has extensive experience in strategic counseling, patent opinion and litigation analysis, as well as trademark, copyright, and trade secret matters.

Distinguished by his demonstrated legal and technical expertise, he has served as trusted counsel for many of the world's premier technology companies.

Over the past decade, Ferrell has presented and spoken about patent and intellectual property issues at legal and technology business forums around the globe. In addition, he is regularly quoted in the media surrounding intellectual property issues including *The Wall Street Journal*, *Business Week*, *Information Week*, *InfoWorld*, *The San Francisco Chronicle*, *California Law Business*, The Recorder, CNN Radio, CNET News, and the Seattle and Silicon Valley/San Jose business journals.